Word

Also by Vivian Cook

Accomodating Brocolli in the Cemetary

All in a
Word

Vivian Cook

MELVILLEHOUSE
BROOKLYN, NEW YORK

Originally published as *It's All in A Word* by Profile Books Ltd, London, 2009

Copyright © Vivian Cook, 2009, 2010

Melville House Publishing
145 Plymouth Street
Brooklyn, New York 11201
mhpbooks.com

ISBN: 978-1-935554-22-6

First Melville House Printing: November 2010
Printed in the United States of America

Typeset in 10.5/13.5pt Minion
Designed by Nicky Barneby @ Barneby Ltd

Library of Congress Control Number: 2010935610

Contents

Introduction

Knowing words

What do we know when we know a word? Clearly we know that the word *dog* means 🐕 or "a four-footed domestic mammal that barks." But any speaker of English knows far more about *dog* than this. Among the things we know about any word are:

- *how to say it or write it* We know that *dog* has three sounds, "d," "o," and "g." If we can read and write, we know also that it has three letters, "d," "o," and "g." A word has its own spoken and written forms, in English connected by complicated spelling rules. Each of us has a mental dictionary telling us how to say or spell each individual word.

- *how to fit it into sentences* We know its part of speech. *Dog* is a noun, meaning that we can use it in the singular for one *dog* and in the plural for many *dogs*; combine it with articles and adjectives, as in *the big dog*; and use it as the subject of sentences, such as *the dog barked*. *Dog* is also a verb meaning "'follow like a dog," as in *the detective dogged his footsteps*, so we can use it in the present tense, *he dogs*, or the past tense, *he dogged*; or add an *-ing* ending, as in *Watson was dogging his footsteps*. All of this information applies to many other English words, as well as *dog*.

   But we also know specifically that the noun *dog* is "countable" rather than "uncountable," meaning that we can say *a dog* and *two dogs*, though we can't say *an air* or *two airs* (except in a specialized sense), because *air* is an uncountable noun. So, our mental dictionary includes information about what kind of noun *dog* is. We also know that the verb *to dog* is likely to have a subject that is animate rather than inanimate: *The police officer dogged him*, not *The bus dogged him*. While the terms seem technical, they're only labels for the knowledge we all have in our mind, which forms the basis for every sentence we say or write.

- *how it combines with other words* We know the typical combinations of words in which *dog* occurs: *go to the dogs*, meaning either "visit a dogtrack" or "deteriorate"; *raining cats and dogs*; *lead a dog's life*; *let sleeping dogs lie*, and dozens more. And we know how *dog* forms compound words to get a distinct meaning: *dog biscuit*, *dog-leg*, *dog tag*, and so on. Knowing a word means knowing its relationships with other words, not just its meaning in isolation: no word is an island.

- *what it means* We know what the word *dog* means. At one level this is a matter of the general meanings that *dog* shares with many other words; a *dog* is concrete rather than abstract like *truth*, animate rather than inanimate like *stone*, animal rather than human like *girl*.

  At another level we know the unique meaning of *dog*, "a four-footed domestic mammal that barks" and have a mental image of a dog 🐕 – whatever distinguishes *dog* from *cat* or from any other animal. But there's more than one meaning to *dog*. It can refer to a person (*dirty dog*), things that fail, ("*That record was a real dog*"), a constellation in the sky (*the dog star*), an instrument with jaws (*iron dog*), and many more.

Our minds contain all this information about the word *dog*. Multiply it by the 60,000 or so words we know and you get some idea of the mammoth store of information about words that we carry around in our mental dictionaries. We don't have just a list of separate words in our minds, each attached to a single meaning. Instead each word radiates into many areas through networks, links, associations, and rules. And this does not take account of the word's history, usually known only to specialists.

All of this information is available to us in a split second when we are speaking or listening. Is *florp* an English word? What about *tedium*? Your reactions were effectively instantaneous; you knew that *tedium* was a word and *florp* wasn't by searching in a fraction of a second through all the words in your mind. Finding the same information in a hardback dictionary would take minutes. Google took 0.03 seconds to find 5,070 examples of *florp*, mostly a username or a nickname, and 0.16 seconds to find a million examples of *tedium*. The same is true of spelling. We speak at up to 200 or so words a minute, 0.3 of a second each. Fran Capo has been timed speaking at 603 words per minute, 0.1 of a second each; needless to say, she is a stand-up comedian. Each word is a package of information that has to be retrieved, sorted out, organized into sentences, and pronounced in 0.3 seconds. The only time we are at all aware of this is when it goes wrong.

What this book is about

This book, then, is all about the different aspects of words, ranging from their forms to their meanings, from their roles in organizing our societies to their roles in helping us to think. It consists of a variety of pieces, some short, some long, some serious, some frivolous, some based on scientific research, some on opinion. As each piece is separate from the others, they can either be dipped into or read consecutively. Similar topics, say children's words or the history of words, are clustered together, though discussions of word forms are spread throughout the book. An Index of themes is given on page 301 to help the reader follow different paths through the book. The book covers familiar topics, such as the history and forms of words, but it also includes less familiar topics, such as how children learn and store words, differences between languages, how words vary from place to place and person to person, and how words shape our mental world. It provides a number of tests to show how many words you know, where you come from, how you learn new words, and so on.

Throughout, the book draws on the ideas of those who have been actively involved in studying and researching words – philosophers, linguists, developmental psychologists and the like, as seen in the list of sources. As with any scientific subject, the study of words tries to explain the facts; the behaviour of words is no more a matter of opinion than the behaviour of electrons. Needless to say, many aspects of words are still little studied, many are controversial, while some of the most important await better techniques for analyzing the brain.

Of course we are all experts about words in the sense that we use them all the time and have strong opinions about them; doubtless my own axes to grind will come across fairly often. The fact that we consist of atoms and have human bodies does not, however, make us physicists or doctors; speaking a human language doesn't qualify us as authorities on language, but it does qualify us to speak about our own experience of it.

1. Thinking in Metaphors?

At school we learn metaphors as part of poetry: "But at my back I always hear/Time's wingèd chariot hurrying near" – something is spoken about as if it were something else. However, according to the linguist George Lakoff, metaphors are not restricted just to poetry but are crucial to our everyday thinking.

Some things are UP	Others are DOWN
happy: "I'm cheering up"	*sad:* "My spirits sank"
conscious: "I woke up"	*unconscious:* "I fell asleep"
in control: "I'm on top of it"	*controlled:* "He's at the bottom of the ladder"
more: "My spirits rose"	*less:* "The Dow fell again"
status: "room at the top"	*lack of status:* "the bottom of the league"
moral: "high-minded"	*immoral:* "low-down trick"

Ideas are	*food:* "I can't digest this theory"
	people: "He's the father of modern linguistics"
	plants: "Physics has many branches"
	products: "Our meeting generated a lot of new ideas"
	knives: "She cut his argument to ribbons"
The mind is	*fragile:* "His mind snapped"
	a machine: "He had a breakdown"
Love is	*war:* "He made many conquests"
	magic: "She entranced me"
	physical force: "fatal attraction"
Time is	*money:* "You spend/waste/save/lose/time"
Understanding is	*seeing:* "I see"
Size is	*importance:* "She's big in the textile industry"

5

There is no intrinsic reason why *happy* should go with up, *love* with magic, and so on. It is just that our minds use metaphors to grapple with the world. Politicians make good use of this, with metaphors such as *the war against terror*, *the fight against drugs*, and *carbon footprint*. In one way such metaphors are justifiable shorthand for complex ideas. But, if they are taken too literally, they become a hindrance rather than a help.

2. Gassers and Slashers

DOCTORS' SLANG

Every group has its own jargon. Sometimes this includes the necessary technical terms that go with the job of being a pilot, a lawyer, and so on. But the jargon also shows that someone belongs to a particular group, whether it's car mechanics, a teenage gang or the conservative Tea Party movement. In addition, euphemisms and black humor are ways of coping with unpleasant or threatening aspects of a job – ways of pretending to have a thick skin. And such jargon can let out repressed feelings that cannot be expressed directly.

Doctors' slang shows all of these effects. Doctors need technical terms, they form a distinct groups and they have to deal with patients in tragic circumstances. Doctors' slang used to be found on actual patients' notes; new openness regulations and people's willingness to sue mean that they are now less likely to be committed to paper. The following examples come from a study by researchers in four English hospitals.

Names of semi-medical conditions

GOK	God only knows
acopia	the inability to cope
cheerioma	a fatal tumor
DOA	dead on arrival
rule of five	A patient's condition is critical if he or she has more than five pieces of equipment attached
LOBNH	lights on but nobody home
TATT	tired all the time
UBI	unexplained beer injury
TEETH	tried everything else, try homeopathy

Medical life

metabolic clinic	the coffee or tea room
ash cash	money for signing cremation forms
the departure lounge	geriatric ward
expensive scare	intensive care
granny dumping	bringing old people into the hospital before bank holidays
feet up general	quiet general hospital
pathology outpatients	the mortuary

Colleagues

Freud Squad, trick cyclists, pest control	psychiatrists
pox docs	staff of the genito-urinary clinic
slashers	surgeons
gassers	anaesthetists
inbred	doctors whose parents were doctors

Patients

crumble, wrinkly, coffin dodger	elderly patient
GROLIES	*Guardian* reader of limited intelligence in ethnic skirt
YSM	yummy scrummy mummy
LOL	little old lady
CLL	chronic low-life
crispy critter	severe burns victim

3. Beatles versus Stones

Beatles songs give the impression that they are about the joys and sorrows of everyday life. Does this effect come from the words they use? Here are the ten most frequent words in twenty-two of their lyrics in order of frequency. The figures are slightly skewed by particular songs, like "Good Day Sunshine."

Most frequent verbs: *love, loves, think, got, make, feel, loving, hold, leaving, send*

Most frequent nouns: *day, home, man, sunshine, eyes, nowhere, ticket, days, girl, week*

Most frequent adjectives: *good, sweet, glad, hard, alone, true, bad, lucky, pretty, tight*

The impression left by Rolling Stones songs is of a tougher, streetwise world. Does that come across from twenty-two of their songs?

Most frequent verbs: *love, hide, taught, like, come, said, rocking, fly, know, make*

Most frequent nouns: *baby, man, cloud, midnight, sparks, gas, name, time, boy, face*

Most frequent adjectives: *wild, sweet, poor, strong, long, round, strange, sick, good, high*

So the Stones are *wild*, the Beatles are *good*. The Stones are *hiding*, *rocking*, and *flying*; the Beatles are *loving*, *feeling*, and *holding*. An overall comparison of these lyrics finds that the main statistical differences are in fact none of these: the Beatles use *she*, *yeah*, *day*, and *good* ("*She loves you, yeah yeah yeah*") far more frequently than the Stones; the Stones use *I* and *get* ("*I can't get no satisfaction*") far more than the Beatles.

4. Making Up Words

Some words have been deliberately created or adapted by particular individuals or organizations.

Kodak: invented by Eastman in 1888; the "k" was supposed to give an impression of strength, as was the pattern "k - - - k"

Xerox: from Greek *xero* (dry) but patterned after Kodak, 1952

gas: invented by Dutch chemist J. B. Van Helmont (1577–1644), apparently from Greek

television: from Greek *tele* (far off) and French *vision;* first found in 1907, even if the first actual transmission took place in 1925. T. S. Eliot considered it an ugly word.

Yahoo: from Swift's race of brutish humans in *Gulliver's Travels*, 1726

Google: from the mathematics term *googol*, meaning an immense number with a hundred zeros after it, invented by a nine-year-old boy

spam: from the canned meat *Spam* (spiced ham), a familiar food in 1940s Britain, revived by the Monty Python sketch "Spam, Spam, lovely Spam"

blurb: derived from Miss Blinda Blurb, a drawing on a book cover by Gelett Burgess in 1907

blatant: from Edmund Spenser's invention *blatant* (bleating?) *beast*, 1596

robot: invented by Karel Čapek in his play *R.U.R.*, 1920

5. How Many Words Do You Know?

BASIC WORDS TEST

A large vocabulary is often taken as a gauge of education and mastery of a language. The Basic Words Test measures the size of your vocabulary against different frequency bands in English. The test first sees whether you know words from the most frequent 1,000 words in English, then from the 1,000–2,000 band, and so on. It goes from the most frequent words down to the least frequent. Definitions have been checked against the *Oxford English Dictionary*. You can expect to know nearly all the words in the first section and fewer and fewer in later sections. Give up when it becomes just guessing.

Complete the definitions below. All the spaces are the same size, so there are no clues to the number of letters. Then check your answers on page 277. The Basic Words Test here tests you up to the 20,000 most frequent words of English. If you get through this with flying colors, try the Advanced Words Test on page 245, which goes beyond the 150,000 level.

Band A: The most frequent 1,000 words

1. a group of people meeting to decide something is a c......................
2. a person who can move heavy objects about is s......................
3. something that many people like is p......................
4. a person who has done well in life is a s......................
5. the group responsible for ruling a country is its g......................
6. a type of building often lived in by a family is a h......................
7. the part of the body that has eyes and is joined to the neck is the h......................

8. something that is consistent with the facts is t........................

9. a room in which paperwork takes place is an o........................

10. to allow something to happen is also to l........................ it happen

Band B: Words up to 3,000 in frequency

11. a round object often used as a toy is a b........................

12. something flexible you carry about and put things in is a b........................

13. to think about past events is to r........................

14. to divide things up among people is to s........................

15. a royal man who rules a country is a k........................

16. to work out the meaning of written words is to r........................

17. a part of the body leading to the foot is a l........................

18. to accept something given to you is to r........................ it

19. when you have evaluated something you have made an a........................

20. to go on with something is to c........................

Band C: Words up to 5,000 in frequency

21. to go from one place to another is to t........................

22. natural, unadulterated food is o........................

23. an elected member of local government is a c........................

24. to look quickly at something is to g........................

25. the opposite of male is f........................

26. to find a new idea or a new place is to d........................it

27. the person who is the best at a competition is the

    c........................

28. a person who works for someone else is an e........................

29. putting forward a new idea is making a s........................

30. a temporary outdoor place for cooking and sleeping is a

    c........................

Band D: Words up to 10,000 in frequency

31. the house or flat where someone lives is their r........................

32. the place where the race ends is the f........................

33. a long object for climbing walls, etc. is a l........................

34. when countries or people refuse to deal with other people
    because they object to their behavior, they are b........................
    them

35. a pipe or artificial channel through which things flow is a

    c........................

36. to give way to someone is to y........................

37. a space without any air is a v........................

38. something that can be carried from place to place is

    p........................

39. getting minerals from the earth is called m........................

40. a man who serves food in a restaurant is a w........................

Band E: Words up to 20,000 in frequency

41. the movement to liberate women is known as f........................

42. a disabled person is sometimes described as h........................

43. a kind of tree with grey bark and winged seeds is an

    a........................

44. one type of British lawyer is called a b........................

45. a person who works without being paid is a v........................

46. a preparation for preventing infectious disease is a

    v.........................

47. something that is not difficult can be called e........................

48. material that you can see through is t........................

49. a kitchen device that cooks by direct heat is a g........................

50. a place known for its health-giving waters is a s........................

6. Car Names

Modern businesses try hard to make the names of their products attractive to potential buyers, none more so than car manufacturers. A study of the American car industry by the linguist Michael Aronoff once found that there were at least five different positions for words in the typical car name, though of course not all of them were used at once.

First comes the year: *a 2006 [model]*
Next comes the make: *a 2006 Ford*
Next the line: *a Ford Galaxy*
Next the model: *a Galaxy economy*
Finally the body type: *a Ford sedan*

Year >	make >	line >	model >	body type
2003	Ford	Focus	compact	Multi-Activity Vehicle
2007	Buick	Enclave	standard	four-door sedan
2008	Honda	CRV	compact	4x4

Devising or advertising a car name means choosing items to fill the different positions: *a 2003 economy sedan*; *a Ford standard coupé* – assuming, of course, that a particular manufacturer makes the whole range. The website for General Motors indeed forces you to choose something for each slot: a make (*Buick, Cadillac, Chevrolet* …), a model (for Buick, *LaCrosse, Enclave,* or *Lucerne*) and a body style (*SUV, pickup, crossover* …)

Choosing one word after another to fill "slots" in the sentence reflects a particular way of constructing sentences from frames with empty slots for words:

| Noun | Verb | Noun |

and then working out which words to fill them with:

| John | likes | beer |
| Jane | likes | John |

For a hundred years this slot-and-filler approach has been a way of teaching languages, called "substitution tables." Students have to make up sentences by choosing words one after the other from left to right

I have some	new	shoes	in my	house
	black	clothes		cupboard
	gray	socks		drawer
	white	stockings		room
	stylish	gloves		
	warm	hats		

so that they can say *I have some stylish clothes in my drawer* or *I have some black shoes in my house* – not very meaningful but helpful as sheer language practice.

One of Noam Chomsky's first contributions to linguistics was an elegant proof that filling slots in a frame doesn't work as a model of how speakers construct sentences. Some choices of words in English are not in sequence from left to right. If you say *Does he like it?*, choosing *does* rather than *do* depends on choosing the singular word *he* (rather than, say, the plural word *they*), which comes after *does* rather than before it. We have to put the sentence together in our minds before we say it, not just choosing one word after another, but paying attention to relationships extending before or after each word.

Nevertheless this process of filling slots with words can be used to produce different phrases: for example, local newspaper headlines:

Column 1	Column 2
Train death	fee
Factory shooting	horror
Horse society funding	failure
School bus	victory

Choose any word from Column 1 and then any from Column 2 to get *factory shooting victory*, *school bus fee*, and so on. Michael Frayn gave precisely this way of producing headlines in one of his novels. Here are some actual local paper headlines that show that the technique is still in use:

Police	hunt	masked man
	stepping up hunt for	missing man
	hunting	window vandal
	hunt for	park raiders
	target	rowdy drunken teens
		bicycle thieves

7. Whose Nickname is That?

Nicknames are alternative means of referring to people or things, usually in a more casual way, often showing the speaker's power over someone else or that they belong to a particular social group. Here is a test of your knowledge of nicknames from different areas of life. The answers are given on page 278. Who is/are:

1. the Artful Dodger ....
2. the President (Prez) ....
3. the Canucks ....
4. the Dean of Swing ....
5. the Red Baron ....
6. the Red Roses ....
7. Buffalo Bill ....
8. the Sun King ....
9. the Cheeseheads ....
10. the Tar Heels ....

Nicknames are often given to newsworthy people, such as:

Sports people: Eddie the Eagle (Edward Edwards, ski-jumper), the Kaiser (Franz Beckenbauer, soccer player), the Sultan of Swat, Babe Ruth (George Herman Ruth, Jr., baseball player), Gorgeous Gussie (Gertrude Moran, tennis player, known for displaying her frilly underwear on court)
Serial murderers: the Boston Strangler, the Yorkshire Ripper, Jack the Ripper, the Zodiac Killer, the Brides in the Night Stalker

The educational researchers Ray Crozier and Patricia Dimmock investigated junior school children's nicknames for each other and came up with the following categories, using the children's own spellings:

Appearance: egghead, wartman, skinny bones, ribs, frekel fase, bag of bones, ginger, fatty, jelly, titch, spotty, bird's nest, scabby lip, chubby, square belly
Psychological attributes: thicko, stupid, dumb, wally, snob
Ethnic group: blacky, gippo
Sexual: bitch, scrubber, tart
Animal: bulldog, rhino, cow, fat dog, Goofy, beast, ant, Dumbo, pig, elephant, Nelly
Nickname related to child's name: banana, Jones bones, zebra

Crozier went on to look at pupils' nicknames for teachers and found most were insults rather than terms of affection:

Appearance: Chewy, Father Christmas, Gorilla, Tintin
Personality: Death Breath, Jaws, Dragon
Other: Herr Owen [Heroin] really screws you up (German teacher), Myrtle the Turtle, Thunder Thighs

The word *nickname* itself shows how a word's form can change due to the way it is perceived. Originally it was *an ekename,* meaning a secondary name, *eke* meaning "also." The "n" was felt to belong to the noun *ekename* rather than to the article *an*, yielding *a nekename*. The same process happened to *an ewt*, based on *an newt*, and in the opposite direction to *an adder*, derived from *a nadder*.

8. Choosing the Right Adjective

WRITERS' WORDS

The ability to choose the right adjective is a necessary attribute of a great poet. Here are the masters' top fifteen in terms of frequency, based on the texts of their main poems.

	Yeats	Eliot	Keats
1.	holy	dry	sweet
2.	crazy	good	light
3.	foul	red	round
4.	young	white	fair
5.	golden	sweet	bright
6.	long	bad	green
7.	mad	free	white
8.	blind	hot	gentle
9.	ill	little	happy
10.	silver	low	little
11.	solid	aetherial	lovely
12.	wild	black	soft
13.	ancient	cold	great
14.	dark	dirty	pleasant
15.	fair	golden	silver

These adjectives are nearly all in everyday use. The only one that stands out as poetic is *aetherial*, meaning "spirit-like," not recorded by the *Oxford English Dictionary* in the twentieth century. They usually have only one or two syllables: *good*, *great*, *bad*, *hot*, *little*, and *lovely*. Many are to do with appearances, such as *golden*, *silver*, *red*, *white*, *black*, *green*, *bright*, and *light*; with sensations, such as *soft*, *cold*, *hot*, and *pleasant*; and with age, such as *young*, *old*, and *ancient*. The poets do not differ much in their choice of adjectives. The giveaways for Yeats are *holy*, *crazy*, and *wild*; for Eliot *dry* (*The Waste Land*); for Keats the cumulative effect of *soft, pleasant, gentle, lovely,* and *happy.*

Are novelists any more adventurous in their choice of adjectives? Here are the top fifteen for three early twentieth-century novelists, D. H. Lawrence (*Sons and Lovers*), James Joyce (*Ulysses*), and P. G. Wodehouse (*My Man Jeeves*).

	Lawrence	Joyce	Wodehouse
1.	good	good	old
2.	dark	little	good
3.	great	new	poor
4.	white	black	new
5.	black	dark	pretty
6.	young	light	young
7.	small	red	great
8.	blue	green	light
9.	cold	blue	glad
10.	warm	lovely	jolly
11.	silent	sweet	red
12.	beautiful	gray	serene
13.	new	cold	wonderful
14.	nice	brown	cold
15.	brown	large	gray

The vocabulary of novelists has many of the same characteristics as that of poets. All the adjectives are monosyllables apart from *lovely, beautiful, silent, wonderful, serene, pretty,* and *jolly.* Many are to do with appearances, such as *white, black, dark, red, blue, gray*; with sensations, *cold, warm,* and *pleasant*; and with age, *young,* and *old.* Nothing stands out – as neutral a set of adjectives as one could imagine. Nine appear among the top fifteen adjectives in the BNC list for English. The missing ones are *different, local, social, important, national, clear,* and *true,* probably not the stuff of novels, or of poetry for that matter.

The emphasis on sight and sensation comes from the need to draw concrete images in readers' minds. The authors rely on familiar adjectives to evoke a particular mental vision.

9. Guessing Games with Words

The object of word guessing games is for players to guess a word or phrase that has been chosen by someone else.

- *In the Manner of the Word:* the group of players sends one person out of the room while they choose an adverb, say *happily*. When the guesser comes back in, he or she asks the others to carry out various actions "in the manner of the word" – "Dance in the manner of the word."

  In a variation called *Dumb Crambo*, the guesser asks questions which must be answered with a rhyming word. Suppose the word is *chair*, the guesser might ask:
  Is it an animal?
  No, it's not a mare.
  Is it food?
  No, it's not a pear.
  In another version, known as *Coffeepot*, the answers have to substitute the word *coffeepot* for the target word, say *banana*:
  Is it big?
  No, coffeepots are quite small.
  Can you buy it in a shop?
  Yes, many shops sell coffeepots.

- *Charades*: a player silently acts out phrases, like *the more the merrier*, film titles, like *Rear Window*, etc. for the rest of the group to guess. Various conventional gestures are sometimes allowed to show if it is a film, a book, or whatever, how many words it has, if it is abbreviated, what the first letter of the word is, and so on.
- *Twenty Questions*, alias *Animal, Vegetable, or Mineral*: people guess a mystery word using up to twenty questions answerable by *Yes* or *No*. The only clue given is whether the word is animal,

vegetable, or mineral (sometimes abstract).

It's vegetable.

Can it be eaten?

Yes.

Does it have to be cooked?

No.

In the variant called *Botticelli*, the player thinks of a famous person, say *Johnny Depp*, and announces the first letter, *D*. The others ask him or her questions and she or he has to reply with the name of another famous person starting with that letter.

Are you a politician?

No, I'm not Bob Dole.

Have you written books?

No, I'm not Charles Dickens.

In another variant called *Twenty Answers* players provide a series of twenty statements that might be answers to questions about the target word and the player has to guess the word.

It's human.

It's part of the body.

It's small.

Twenty Questions exploits the type of meaning that uses a set of plus or minus features – edible [+], cooked [-], as discussed on pages 77–88 can you narrow down the choices to just one word by having twenty yes (+) or no (-) pieces of information? For this reason it is easy to devise a computer program that "learns" from examples that are fed into it and soon becomes almost unbeatable – a commercial version is on sale.

10. Superheroes in Cyberspace
SCIENCE FICTION WORDS

Science fiction writers have enriched English with many words or meanings of words that are found for the first time in their writings, such as William Gibson's *Cyberspace*. *Grok*, invented by Robert Heinlein in 1961, appears on the Brown list of the most frequent 2000 words of English – because their sample included Heinlein's *Stranger in a Strange Land*.

airlock, 1928, Doc Smith
blast off, 1937, Doc Smith
cyberspace, 1982, William Gibson
Dalek, 1963, Terry Nation
deep space, 1937, Doc Smith
force field, 1931, Doc Smith
humanoid, 1940, Isaac Asimov
hyperspace, 1931, John Campbell (1909 in maths)
offworld, 1957, Andre Norton
parallel universe, 1923, H. G. Wells
planet Earth, 1941, *Comet* magazine
space warp, 1935, N. Schachner
spaceman, 1933, C. L. Moore
spaceworthy, 1931, Doc Smith
starbase, 1944, R. M. Williams
starship, 1934, F. Kelly
subspace, 1940, A. E. van Vogt
superhero, 1942, *Superspine* comics
teleportation, 1951, John Wyndham
terraform, 1942, Jack Williamson
time machine, 1895, H. G. Wells
vacuum suit, 1947, N. Schachner
Venusian, 1874, Anne Blair

11. What Does a Word Mean?

It seems easy enough to say what a word means. *Sun* means ✹, *car* means 🚗. But 🚗 is a picture of a *car*, not a real car; we can look at ✹, but not at the real sun. This is the same point made by René Magritte's picture of a pipe labelled *Ceci n'est pas une pipe* (This is not a pipe). A picture is not the real thing: a map is not the land it represents. When a woman told Magritte that the arm of a woman in one of his paintings was too long, he answered, "Madam, you are mistaken. That is not a woman, it is a painting."

Does *car* then mean an actual car rather than a picture of a car? If *car* meant a concrete individual car, each separate car in the world would have a unique name, rather like the number plate which assigns each car a unique identity. Instead the word car means the concept of a car, i.e. cars in general. What counts is the idea of a car, relating to all cars rather than to any car in particular, so that you can see a Bugatti or a Beetle, a gleaming limousine or an old junker, and say "That's a car" if it fits your idea of carness.

The word *car* links something that exists in the world with a concept in our minds. There's no way of linking the word and the world without the mind. Cars don't usually come labelled as *cars*; it's us who call them *cars*. The word *car* shows how a speaker of English organizes the world – it's not a *bus* and it's not a *bike* – by relating a meaning inside her mind to something outside. When we say that a word refers to something – *car* refers to 🚗 – we are taking a short cut that leaves out the mind in between.

The actual object doesn't have to have a concrete existence. Unicorns and Martians exist only in pictures, but there are words for them and people have a good image of what unicorns look like, if perhaps not Martians. Words like *truth*, *globalization*, and *education* are abstract; at best we can give examples of true things, of globalization, or of education, but we can't point at something clearly labelled *truth*. The objects do not even have to pretend to exist – we can after all talk about *nothing* or *the square root of minus one*, which has no existence at all. Words are clumps of information that represent our mental concept, whether relating to real or imaginary things.

Nor is the physical world cut up into separate objects, each of which has a word to label it. Instead it is parcelled up by the words of our language. Standard English has only two words for grandparents, *grandmother* and *grandfather*. Languages like Swedish have distinct words for your father's parents, *farfar* and *farmor*, and your mother's parents, *morfar* and *mormor*. Standard English recognizes fewer complex family relations than do many other languages.

Since all human beings live in rather similar physical worlds, they need many words for roughly the same things. We all need words for the sun and the moon, for food and drink, for mother and son, and so on. The fact that different languages have words for the same things reflects the common ways in which human beings organize their mental worlds. But even common things can be perceived quite differently. Speakers of Hopi, an indigenous American language, don't have a single word for "water" but have different words for water in a lake, *kehi*, and for water to drink, *pahe*. Japanese doesn't have a single word for rice but different words for raw rice, *kome*, cooked rice, *gohan*, fried rice, *yakimeshi*, and rice cooked to accompany western dishes, *raisu*.

So there are enormous problems in translating from one language to another. You naturally expect to find a word in another language that is an exact equivalent to yours. But translating English *rice* into Japanese means deciding whether the rice is raw, cooked or served with western dishes. Many languages have an everyday word for "children of the same parent," *Geschwister* in German; English has only an academic term, *sibling*, rather than an everyday word. So how do you translate *Wieviel Geschwistern haben Sie?* – *How many X do you have?* Translating it as *How many siblings do you have?* makes it sound like academic research rather than ordinary conversation. The only real possibility is to change it into *How many brothers and sisters do you have?*, the closest English can get to it, by spelling out the concept in several words.

This came home to me during an experiment that involved people counting backwards aloud in various languages. Some Japanese participants asked me what seemed a curious question: "What am I supposed to be counting?" I was soon told that there are different number words in Japanese according to what you are counting: *hitotsu*, one, *futatsu*, two, and *mittsu*, three, can be used up to ten for ordinary objects such as books but cannot be used for people. Often you need to add a special classifier according to whether it is an animal, a long thin object, and so on.

The nearest equivalents in English are the names for groups of things – a *pride of lions*, a *pack of wolves*, a *bouquet of flowers*. Mastering counting in Japanese also means learning that the word for four, *shi*, has to be avoided as it happens to have the same pronunciation as the word for death.

So even a simple activity like counting reflects the language we speak. Our concepts and our vocabulary have a symbiotic relationship. A new idea needs a new word; the word *iPod* wasn't needed until the gadget was invented. To be more than a sequence of nonsense sounds, a new word needs a meaning; making up the word *flink* is useless unless I have something to use it for, some meaning to convey for which no existing word will do.

Some concepts are intrinsic to the workings of our mind. A Polish linguist who works in Australia, Anna Wierzbicka, has spent her life researching universals of meaning that occur in all human languages, and has come up with sixty or so elements in fifteen groups. One group is *I, you, someone, something, people, body*; another is *live, die*; another *kind of, part of* (see page 272). These are the basic sixty ideas that all human beings share and for which they all need words.

The fact that all human beings share a particular meaning still does not explain why they need it. Why should we all want to talk about *I* and *live*? It could be our shared human situation; we all live and die so we all need to talk about the experience. Or it could be hardwired into our brains; we say *kind of* and *part of* because our brains work by dividing things up, just as underlying the most sophisticated computer routine is a binary sequence of "0"s and "1"s.

It is almost impossible to decide whether we can think without words. For we necessarily have to turn the thoughts into words to be able to handle them better or to talk to other people. Even if there is a stratum of the mind where concepts are separate from language, how could we tell other people about it without passing through language?

12. Cooking with Words

Words are linked to each other in many ways. Take verbs for cooking. The linguist Adrienne Lehrer showed how the English words for cooking fit together, going from words with the broadest meaning at the top to those with the most precise meaning at the bottom.

cook							
boil		fry		grill		bake	
simmer	(full) boil	sauté	deep-fry	grill	barbecue	bake	roast

For English speakers the verb *cook* covers a range of different cooking processes, such as *boiling* (with water), *frying* (with oil, etc.), *grilling* (direct heat without liquid), and *baking* (enclosed heat without liquid). Each of these is mutually exclusive. If you are *boiling*, you're not *frying*; you can't fry and grill at the same time, even if you're Heston Blumenthal or the Iron Chef.

Each of these activities can be broken up further. *Boiling* can be either *simmering* (gentle) or *full boiling* (fierce). *Frying* can be *sautéing* or *deep-frying*. *Grilling* has a variant, *barbecuing*. *Baking* is also called *roasting*. Again, if you are *grilling*, you're not *barbecuing*; if you're *sautéing*, you're not *deep-frying*. Each word has its own territory.

Some words are nevertheless ambiguous: an ox is *roasted* on a spit, but meat or potatoes are *roasted* in the oven, two rather different cooking methods. And British cooks have some different words from American ones: *broiling* on one side of the Atlantic is *grilling* on the other; the American terms for fried eggs like *over easy* and *sunnyside up* are baffling to British people; the concept of a *joint* as a large piece of meat seems peculiarly British. A few basic cooking words cover much of what we need to say by dividing up the general area of cooking into more and more specific areas.

While most of these cooking activities happen anywhere in the world, languages divide up the activity of cooking differently in words. The diagram below, based on Lehrer's research, shows the divisions of Japanese cookery, where the main category is *ryori*, or food preparation (Lehrer called this *nitaki* but Japanese friends assure me the correct term now is *ryori*). The overall concept of cooking in Japanese, *ryori*, divides up into *niru*, boiling, which has two subdivisions, *yuderu*, boiling, and *taku*, cooking over heat, usually boiling rice – not particularly needed in the West; *musu*, steaming; *ageru*, deep-frying; and *yaku*, baking, roasting, grilling and frying with fat, which in turn is subdivided into *itameru*, stir-fry with a small amount of fat in a frying pan, *iru*, stir-fry small pieces of food or roast nuts and seeds, without fat, and *aburu*, which involves direct heat. The Japanese clearly cook a bit differently.

cook: *ryori*						
boil: *niru*		steam *musu*	deep-fry *ageru*	bake, roast, grill, fry: *yaku*		
boil *yuderu*	boil rice *taku*			stir-fry *itameru*	*iru*	*aburu*

Japanese people have another dimension of cookery barely covered in English, namely, the preparation of uncooked foods such as *sushi* and *sashimi*. English doesn't allow us to say we cook the salad unless we apply heat to it; we have to step outside basic cooking vocabulary and say *I prepared/made/dressed the salad*. It is not just that there are different recipes in different countries; people think about food in different ways.

Areas of the world and of life get divided up by the words we use, and these divisions differ from one language to another. Examples given elsewhere in this book are the ways languages divide up a family into relatives and divide up the colors of the spectrum with words. Our vocabulary reflects how we live and the way we see the world.

To test your knowledge of world cuisine: In which English-speaking countries are these cookery terms chiefly used? Answers and definitions on page 279.

1. Fiddleheads ....
2. Pasty ....
3. Candy ....
4. Poutine ....
5. Chook ....
6. Garbanzos ....
7. Etouffée ....
8. Skillet ....
9. Copha ....
10. To shred ....
11. Mushy peas ....
12. Tourtière ....
13. Farina ....
14. Cilantro ....
15. Roast potatoes ....

13. Fardling Gwiks
STRUCTURE VERSUS CONTENT WORDS

English words fall into two broad types: those that belong in the dictionary, like *storm* and *confabulate*, called content words, and those that belong in the grammar, like *of* and *the*, called structure words or function words. To see the difference, here is a quotation from a Theodore Sturgeon story using made-up content words but real structure words:

So on Lirht, while the decisions on the fate of the miserable Hvov were being formulated, gwik still fardled, funted and fupped.

If the same sentence were done with made-up structure words and real content words, it might have read:

So kel Mars, dom trelk decisions kel trelk fate mert trelk miserable slaves hiv polst formulated, deer still grazed, jumped kosp survived.

The version with made-up content words is comprehensible to some extent; we have some idea of what is going on because we know how the words are connected even if we do not know exactly what fardling and funting are. The version with made-up structure words is almost incomprehensible, even though we know what grazing and jumping are; we can't connect the words.

Some of the main differences between structure and content words are:

- Content words consist of Nouns (*glass*), Verbs (*move*), Adjectives (*glossy*) etc.; structure words consist of Prepositions (*to*), Articles (*the*), Auxiliaries (*can*) etc. In other words, content words and structure words belong to different parts of speech.
- For this reason, content words, such as *book*, *teddy bear*, and

encapsulate, are listed and explained in the dictionary; structure words are explained in the grammar book in terms of rules for fitting them into phrases and sentences: *the*, for instance, is a definite article going with nouns.

- Any speaker of English always pronounces and spells content words in virtually the same way; *tree* always has the same consonants and vowels. Structure words, on the other hand, change their pronunciation for emphasis, etc.; *am* can be said as "am" when stressed *I am mad at him*, or as "m" when unstressed, *I'm mad at him*; the indefinite article *a* varies between "uh" and "ay" (the sound in *day*) depending whether it is stressed: *This is a book about China/This is a book about China.*

- In terms of spelling, content words usually have more than two letters, as in *eye, two, inn*; structure words may have only one or two letters, as in *I, to, in*. This so-called three-letter rule works pretty well, despite exceptions, such as the two-letter content word *go* and the eight-letter structure word *although*.

- There are large numbers of content words, tens or hundreds of thousands, as seen in any dictionary. Structure words are comparatively few in number, consisting of 220 or so in English, such as *the, he, to, with, by, though, that, where, I*, etc.

- Words that start "th" are pronounced with a voiceless "th" when they are content words: *think, theme, theory*, but with a voiced "th" when they are structure words: *this, the, there*.

- Content words usually have the same stress pattern whenever they are said: "theater" is always *theater* never *theater*. Structure words are usually unstressed but can be stressed for emphasis: *I'll do it/I will do it, I have done it/I have done it.*

- It is always possible to invent a new content word – I heard *vagueity* on the radio this morning. Virtually all the new words coming into the language, such as *cyberpunk*, are content words. Structure words can never be invented, as witness the failed attempt to replace *he/she* with the gender-neutral *per*, seen in Marge Piercy's novel *Woman on the Edge of Time*. Any change in structure words takes place over a long period of time – Old

English *heo* and *hem* became Modern English *she* and *them* (which is incidentally why the form *'em* in *Give 'em hell* is historically a case of h-dropping, not of th-dropping).

- Structure words are mostly very high frequency, such as *the* and *to*; all the ten commonest words in English are structure words, as are forty-five of the top hundred words.

The difference between structure words and content words has been important for language teachers and has implications for many areas of English. Naturally, linguists describing English grammar have more complex analyses as the distinction doesn't always work well. For example, while prepositions like *in* and *to* are called structure words, they behave in many ways like content words and are treated as such in some schools of grammatical analysis.

14. Gender and First Name

Which of these names – some real, some invented – do you think is more likely to be a man's name or a woman's name? Underlining means the syllable is stressed.

	man's name	woman's name
1. <u>Re</u>fel	☐	☐
2. Ronk	☐	☐
3. <u>Bro</u>lay	☐	☐
4. Pam	☐	☐
5. Pom<u>set</u>	☐	☐
6. Teplee	☐	☐
7. Corlak	☐	☐
8. Ringo	☐	☐
9. June	☐	☐
10. Pon<u>veen</u>	☐	☐
11. Tony	☐	☐
12. Derleeg	☐	☐
13. Anita	☐	☐
14. Renfandix	☐	☐
15. Foop	☐	☐
16. Pelcra	☐	☐
17. Falrobin	☐	☐
18. Tom	☐	☐
19. Melissa	☐	☐
20. Len	☐	☐

The underlying idea is that there is a gender pattern to English first names. Certain sounds and letters go with men's names, others go with women's names, depending on:

- **how many syllables are there in the word**
  Men's names typically have fewer syllables than women's. So the made-up names *Foop* (15) and *Ronk* (2) are likely to be men's names, *Falrobin* (17) and *Renfandix* (14) women's names. Out of the real names, *Tom* (18) and *Len* (20) are typical short men's names, *Anita* (13) and *Melissa* (19) typical long women's names. *Tony* (11) and *Ringo* (8) are slightly long for men's names, *June* (9) and *Pam* (4) slightly short for women's names.
- **where the stress comes in the word**
  Men's names are typically stressed on the first syllable, women's names on the second. So the made-up names *Refel* (1) and *Brolay* (3) with initial stress sound more like male names than *Ponveen* (10) and *Pomset* (5) with stress on the second syllable.
- **whether the name ends in a consonant or a vowel**
  Women's names tend to end in a vowel, men's names in a consonant. The invented *Pelcra* (16) and *Teplee* (6) are more likely to be women's names than *Corlak* (7) and *Derleeg* (12).

Anita (13) and *Melissa* (19) are typical women's names, having both more than one syllable and a final vowel, while *Len* (20) and *Tom* (18) are typical men's names with one syllable and a final consonant. *Tony* (11) and *Ringo* (8) are unusual men's names in having two syllables and ending in vowels, *June* (9) and *Pam* (4) are unusual women's names in having one syllable and ending in a consonant.

Fantasy Character Names

Test this out on some of the characters in the George Martin fantasy series *A Song of Ice and Fire*. Answers on page 279.

	man's name	woman's name
1. Devan	☐	☐
2. Sansa	☐	☐
3. Mance	☐	☐
4. Brienne	☐	☐
5. Cersei	☐	☐
6. Walder	☐	☐
7. Rylene	☐	☐
8. Cotter	☐	☐
9. Daenerys	☐	☐
10. Tyrion	☐	☐
11. Emphyiria	☐	☐
12. Asha	☐	☐
13. Loras	☐	☐
14. Tarle	☐	☐
15. Annara	☐	☐
16. Rollam	☐	☐
17. Alayaya	☐	☐
18. Sarella	☐	☐
19. Clegane	☐	☐
20. Ragwyle	☐	☐

If you could guess these correctly, it shows how closely the names that authors make up for fantasy fiction still resemble English. And of course the patterns of English are themselves derived from historical relationships with other languages, such as the final feminine ending -*a* in some Latin names.

15. Words with Many Meanings
THE CASE OF "HOUSE"

Much of the time we treat each word as if it had a single meaning: *cat* means 🐈 "feline quadruped." But *cat* also means a "spiteful person" or a "jazz fan" and is short for *catalytic converter*, *catamaran* and *computer-assisted tomography* (*CAT scan*). Similarly, *bank* obviously means "a place to keep your money." Well, these days *riverbanks* and *sandbanks* might keep it safer.

All the different meanings of a single word might be spinoffs from some basic central sense; if you know this, you can work out all the others. A *cat* is a "spiteful person" because cats hiss at people, but what is a *cool cat*? It is difficult to link the meanings of *bank* because they come in two sets: those derived from "raised ground" as in *bank of clouds*, and those related to *bench*, "sitting place" (where moneylenders traded and judges still preside). It is more or less coincidence that both meanings ended up attached to the same word, *bank*. The dictionary makers have claimed that the main lesson of extensive computer research with vocabulary is that words do not have central meanings, just many different meanings.

Counting the number of words in a dictionary gives us little idea of how many words speakers know; the real question is, How many meanings? But that all depends on how you count them – the *Oxford English Dictionary* (*OED*) has three main entries and twenty-seven subentries for *bank*, before you reach compounds like *bank balance* or *bank clerk* or phrases like *cry all the way to the bank*. One word? Three words? Or twenty-seven words that happen to have the same pronunciation and spelling?

Let us see how this works out with a single word, *house*. *House* is among the 300 most used words of English. The *OED*, the most complete source for English, has forty-three pages of printout for *house* in the online version, with nine main entries and twenty-four subentries if you include phrases. The meaning of what the

OED calls "the simple word" *house* is given as "a building for human habitation; esp. a building that is the ordinary dwelling place of a family": people by and large live in houses.

But do they actually have to live there? A *lighthouse* is for displaying a warning light and may or may not be inhabited. A *public house* is for drinking, even if some of its patrons appear never to leave. The *Houses of Parliament* are not a place for British politicians to live, even if some go to sleep there. In other words, a *house* can be a place where people gather in groups for a purpose. A whole group of meanings to do with "belonging to an establishment" spins off from this, such as *house wine* in restaurants, *house lights* in a theater or *house band* in clubs, together with such jobs as a *housekeeper* and a *housemaid*.

Do the residents of a house have to be human beings? A *warehouse* is for storing goods; a *hothouse* for keeping plants. *House* also means something that purposefully contains something – *Put the tool back in its house*. The residents of the house, so to speak, are anything that belongs within a house, whether a *houseplant*, a *housefly*, or a *house mite*, though *house sparrows* and *house martins* are not usually welcome indoors.

Does a house have to have a physical location? Schools can have *houses* that pupils belong to even if the buildings don't exist. A business can be a *publishing house* without anyone imagining that it is run from the publisher's home; some business tasks may be carried out *in house* rather than farmed out to others. A *house* can be an invisible, notional place.

Does it have to be a place at all? A *house* is also a group of people: the *House of Windsor* or the *House of Saud*. One meaning is any group linked by some common theme, such as a family.

And there are many more meanings, such as *House of God, house of the ascendant* (astrology) and *house music*. In the compound words with *house*, the meaning can seldom be worked out from the sum of the parts: *a hothouse* is not the same as a house that is hot, and *a glasshouse* is more likely to have bars, at least in the Army, than glass in its windows.

The number of meanings for the common word *house* and its compounds is at least in the hundreds without going outside everyday meanings all of us are familiar with: one simple word has multiple meanings. Doubtless the same is true for virtually every word in the language. What each of us knows about words is mind-boggling in its extent. Yet we instantly handle all these meanings as we speak and write, understanding and producing the words in split seconds.

16. Words in the Blender

A blend is when two words are put together to make a new word: *net* is combined with *etiquette* to get *netiquette*. Some blends are the deliberate invention of a single individual: Lewis Carroll put *snort* together with *chuckle* to get *chortle*: "*Callooh! Callay!*"/*He chortled in his joy.*" In this case he added a new word to the language, though other new words in the same poem *Jabberwocky*, have not been adopted into everyday use, such as *slithy* and *whiffled*.

Regardless of who actually invents the word, blending is one of the processes at work in the development of a language over time. Some of the ways of creating blends are:

- **overlapping** – the two words share a bit in the middle: filmania (fil[m] mania), netiquette
- **clipping** – parts of the words are left out
  1. a whole word plus part of a second
     fanzine (fan [maga]zine), babelicious (babe [de]licious), travelogue (travel [dial]ogue), bankster (bank [gang]ster)
  2. part of the first word plus the whole of the second
     Eurasia (Eur[ope] asia), alcopop (alco[holic] pop), Britpop (Brit[ish] pop)
  3. the first part of the first word is added to the last part of the second
     smog (sm[oke] [f]og), electrocute (electr[ic] [exe]cute), camcorder (cam[era] [re]corder), brunch (br[eakfast] [l]unch), Spam (sp[iced] [h]am), chunnel (ch[annel] [t]unnel), heliport (heli[copter] [air]port)
  4. the first parts of both words are combined
     agitprop (agit[ate] prop[aganda]), modem (mo[dulator] dem[odulator])
  5. miscellaneous
     blog ([we]b log), podcast ([i]Pod [broad]cast)

- **clipping at boundaries within words:** Oxbridge (Ox[ford] [Cam]bridge)
- **clipping and overlapping:** motel (mo[tor] [ho]tel)
- **imperfect overlapping:** chump (ch[unk] [st]ump)

Blends are also produced spontaneously when we speak, as in the following examples discussed by psycholinguists:

That's torrible (terrible + horrible)
Have you ever flivven (flown + driven)
grastly (grizzly + ghastly)

Spontaneous blends are signs of how people produce speech. If you can't make up your mind which of two words to say, you produce a blend of both.

17. Soft, Mellow, Fragrant, and Sweet
ALCOHOLIC WORDS

In a famous cartoon, James Thurber had a character describe a wine as follows: "It's a naive domestic Burgundy without any breeding, but I think you'll be amused by its presumption." Talking about wine involves a host of specialized and non-specialized vocabulary, as described by the linguist Adrienne Lehrer.

Here are four of the scales she used. Any wine can be described by choosing the right word from each of the scales.

–		Sweetness		+
syrupy	sweet	semi-sweet	dry	bone dry
cloying				
sugary				

In this scale only the left-hand column is negative in meaning: *syrupy* is terrible; a wine can't be too dry – *bone dry* is great!

–		Feel		+
hard	puckery	firm		soft
harsh				smooth
sharp				velvety
rough				silky
bitter				gentle
				tender
				mellow

The scale goes from flavors that are bad on the left – you don't want a wine that is *harsh* and *bitter* – to good on the right – a *gentle, mellow* wine is something to look forward to. *Puckery* is not necessarily a bad thing, it seems. Note that *hard* is bad but *firm* is good!

Age

–	+		–
green	young fresh	mature	old withered dead
unripe		ripe	dying
immature		mellow	decrepit
		developed	senile
		evolved	
		aged	

This scale is best in the middle, i.e. just the right age, with too young on the left – *green* – and too old on the right – *decrepit*. The best age varies according to the wine; a *mature* wine is probably better than a *young* one.

Nose

+	–
fruity	grapy (nasty smells) musty, yeasty
flowery	(comparisons) burnt
perfumed	rubber, leather
scented	
fragrant	
smoky	
(specific fruits) cherries, raspberries	

Nose means the smell of the wine. Perhaps because of a lack of words for describing smell, many of these compare the wine to other things – *fruit, old socks* etc. It's a good wine that smells *fragrant* and *smoky*, a dud wine if it's *leathery* and *musty*.

To sound like a wine expert, simply choose one word from each scale – *a syrupy, hard, immature wine that smells of leather*, say. There are another eight scales, so your expertise does not go very far.

To make your wine talk sound more convincing, you could always throw in the odd term used by wine scientists, such as *buttery, clean, complex, foxy, gassy, maderized, oaky, peppery, sound, tannic, young. Maderized* sounds particularly convincing. In case anyone challenges you, it means "brown from oxygen and age." Or indeed you could venture into more esoteric terms, such as *estery* and *malo-lactic.*

So that this is not too biased towards wine drinkers, here is a selection of terms for whisky taken from the bottlings list of the Scottish Malt Whisky Society. How about a drop of *straw-colored, buttery equinoctial* this evening?

assertive	astringent	biscuit
bitter	bronze	buttery
chewy	clean	complex
crisp	damp	dry
equinoctial	filling	fine
fruity	full	gentle
heavy	intense	large
malty	mellow	medicinal
mild	mouldy	oleaginous
pale	peaty	peppery
phenolic	powerful	pungent
red-gold	rewarding	rich
robust	salty	sharp
sherried	shiny	simple
smoky	smooth	sour
spicy	spirituous	stalwart
straw-colored	strong	sulphurous
sweet	tart	uncomplicated

And now for the beer drinkers, who's for *a pint of spicy chewy bitter with a rocky head and a hint of lychees*? Here are words to describe the four most important elements of a beer.

Head: *dense, thin, rocky, sparse, thick, creamy, firm*
Aroma: *malt, dark/roasted/burnt chocolate, coffee, spicy, pine, hoppy, banana nose, pungent, warming*

Mouth-feel: *silky, smooth, dry, thick, chewy, thin, fizzy, soft, full, watery, grainy*

Flavor: *hoppy, grapefruit, vanilla, chocolaty, syrupy, bittersweet, rich, crisp, lychee, biscuit, mocha coffee, stone fruit, smoky*

18. Of Mice and Mouses

ENGLISH PLURALS

English nouns usually have both singular and plural forms, *apple* and *apples*. The "regular" plural is spelled with "s," *books*, or "es," *batches*, and pronounced as "s," *chairs*, as "z," *times*, or as "iz," *grasses*.

But many words have irregular plural forms, i.e. ones that do not fit these rules. The reason is often that they originally came from another language. When they entered English, they sometimes carried over the original plural form, as in *spaghetti*, and sometimes created English plurals, *formulas*. And of course some are hotly disputed while they are undergoing this process – *gladioli* or *gladioluses*?

- Latin is one key source, dating back to the long centuries when it was the language of the educated elite across Europe. *Stimulus/stimuli* and *larva/larvae* have kept their Latin plurals. *Crocus* is still in the process of switching from *croci* to *crocuses*, as are *gladiolus* (*gladioli/gladioluses*) and *fungus* (*fungi/funguses*). *Area* and *drama* have completed the switch to English plurals, *areas* and *dramas*. Indeed, people sometimes invent new "Latin" plurals, such as the many examples of *formuli* that can be found on Google.
- Greek had a similar impact through academic words: *crisis/crises* and *phenomenon/phenomena*. Many of these now have only English plurals, such as *electron/electrons*.
- French contributed some words where the plural is spelled with an "x" but pronounced as a "z": *bureaux* and *adieux*. However, many words have made the switch completely, such as *plateau/plateaus*.

Some odd plurals survive from pre-Norman Conquest Old English: *children, oxen, brethren*. Old English is also the source of plurals with consonant changes, like *half/halves*, with vowel changes, *woman/women* and *foot/feet*, and when nothing changes: *sheep/sheep*.

When a word with an irregular plural is given a new meaning, it often takes a regular plural. So, although *leaves* is the usual plural of *leaf*, the Toronto hockey team is called the *Maple Leafs*, a tea in Taiwan is called *Leafs* and a Swedish band is called *Fallen Leafs*. The normal irregular plural for *mouse* must be *mice*, yet *computer mice* gives a strange image of little creatures dashing about the mouse-pad rather than the new regular plural, *computer mouses*; nevertheless, Dell computers use *mice* on their website. If you have more than one *BlackBerry*, do you have two *BlackBerries* or two *BlackBerrys*? Interestingly the same regularization effect applies to the pronunciation of irregular spellings: *salmon* is said without an "l" but *salmonella* clearly has one.

The two processes for forming plurals have provided insights for psycholinguists investigating how the mind handles language. One view is that language consists of a few rules, so that making words plural simply involves adding *-s* or *-es*. Another is that knowing a language means remembering thousands of examples, in this case that plurals are *books, mice, batches, men*, etc. The linguist Steven Pinker uses plurals as a test case of rules versus examples. We won't get very far with English if we don't know how to make plurals by rule, say for new words – *one iPhone, two…*? But we still need to remember a few hundred one-off plurals like *children, schemata*, and *crises*. In other words, language is made up of both rules and examples, not just one or the other. Children have to learn not only the overall rules of English but also thousands of examples where the rules don't apply, perhaps most obviously in spelling.

19. Common Words

To check your idea of word frequency, before reading on, write down the three commonest words of English in each of these categories:

- words in general: ....
- nouns: ....
- verbs: ....
- adjectives: ....

Frequency is involved in the study of words in many ways. The question is often not so much whether someone has ever uttered a particular word – try typing any random sequence of letters into Google and you find it exists somewhere on the Web – but how often people use it. *Immunosurveillance* is in the *Oxford English Dictionary* but it doesn't occur once in the British National Corpus (BNC) of 100 million running words.

Here are the most common content words from the BNC:

	Nouns	Verbs	Adjectives
1.	year	say	new
2.	time	know	good
3.	people	get	old
4.	way	go	different
5.	government	see	local
6.	day	make	small
7.	man	think	great
8.	world	take	social
9.	work	come	important
10.	life	use	national

People's off-the-cuff guesses about high-frequency words might include *man* and *day* among the top ten, but who would guess *government* and *world*? These frequencies are different from those used in teaching English to non-native speakers, which tend to start from concrete visualizable words like *house* and *chair* rather than abstractions like *year* and *work*, partly because they are easier to teach.

All English texts have common characteristics. The following list shows the most frequent words in the BNC, the writing of seven-year-old children, the narrative parts of Jane Austen's novels, and the writing of Japanese learners of English.

	BNC	7-year-old children	Jane Austen	Japanese learners
1.	the	and	the	I
2.	of	the	to	to
3.	and	a	and	the
4.	a	I	of	you
5.	in	to	a	and
6.	to	was	her	a
7.	it	it	I	my
8.	is	he	was	in
9.	was	we	in	it
10.	I	in	it	for

The columns look very similar. *The* is in the top three on all four lists; *of, and, a, to, I* and *it* feature in all the lists, *was* in all the lists but one. All of these are structure words – the words like *of* and *the* that glue the content words – nouns, verbs, etc. – of English together into phrases and sentences (see page 33). Whoever you are, whatever you are writing about, you make use of the same high-frequency structure words. Yet they don't come to mind as common words. Structure words are effectively invisible to us compared to nouns and verbs; in a sense we don't see them as words. All the top hundred words in English in the BNC are structure words apart from *time, said, now, people, new, years, way* and the numbers *one, two, first*. About 45 percent of the running words in any piece of English writing come from the top hundred. In other words, knowing a hundred words lets you recognize nearly half the words you meet in English.

20. Nicknames Rule!

THE POWER OF NICKNAMES

Elizabeth Taylor? Liz Taylor? Lizzie Taylor? What's the difference?

Making a nickname by shortening the first name is easy enough – *Peter* to *Pete*, *Gabriel* to *Gabe*, *Andrew* to *Andy* or *Drew*, depending where you come from. Adding *-ie* or *-y*, as in *Nicky*, *Bobbie*, and *Frankie*, is another way of creating a nickname. In many languages the "high" "i" vowel by itself suggests smallness, as in *teeny* or *wee beastie*, compared to the "low" vowels that suggests bigness in *huge* and *large* (see page 112). While adding an "i" sound to someone's name sounds familiar and friendly, it also hints that they are small and childish. Rightly is *-ie/-y* called the diminutive ending – it cuts you down to size.

Shortening someone's name or adding *-ie/-y* gives away your attitude to them: *Nick/Nicky*, *Ed/Eddie*, *Alf/Alfie*. Short forms like *Tom* sound slightly less condescending than *-ie/-y* forms like *Tommy*. In a backlash against *-ie/-y*, some nicknames have "y"-less endings, such as *Johnno* for *Johnny*, *Anders* for *Andrew*, *Debs* for *Debbie* or *Kell* for *Kelly*.

People change their nickname to suit their status. Jazz altoist *Johnny Dankworth* became respectable *Sir John Dankworth*. The trend toward the full name has in recent times been partly reversed, as with *Bill Clinton*. Even the *-ie/-y* forms have become more frequently used. While in the 1950s the prime minister was definitely *Anthony* Eden, in the 1980s *Maggie* was prime minister in some contexts, and the leader of "New" Labour was definitely *Tony*.

Sometimes the nickname appears to have little to do with the real name – what has *Jack* got to do with *John*? A former professor at Essex University was named *Arthur Spicer* but used the name *Sam*. One of his ex-students assumed this was a general rule and wrote a textbook for English, which asserted that "In England all *Arthurs* are known as *Sam*."

There is a widespread belief that knowing someone's name gives you power over them – witness any novel about vampires. Using the first name is one signal of power, whether from teacher to pupil or boss to secretary, or echoed in newspapers' use of first names and nicknames for female victims of crimes – *Jackie's body found*. A mild form of this is the power to give people nicknames. Shortening the name *Susan* to *Sue* shows familiarity; adding an *-ie/-y* shows an additional layer of condescension, *Susan* to *Susie*.

The Friendliness Scale

Check off politicians on the scale of friendliness according to whether you have heard them referred to by the possible nicknames on the list.

	Distant		Fairly Friendly		Friendly	
Rice	Condoleezza	☐	Condi	☐	Connie	☐
Bush	George W.	☐	Dubya	☐	Georgie	☑
Sarkozy	Nicolas	☐	Nick	☐	Nicky	☐
Thatcher	Margaret	☐	Maggie	☐	Mags	☐
Churchill	Winston	☐	Winnie	☐	Win	☐
Blair	Anthony	☐	Tony	☐	Tone	☐
Cameron	David	☐	Dave	☐	Davey	☐

21. Levels of Meaning

The psychologist Eleanor Rosch suggested that there are three levels of meaning:

- **a basic level** consisting of words for common everyday things – *potato* and *car*
- **a superordinate level** of more abstract words that group things together – *vegetable* for *potato*, *spinach*, and *motor vehicle* for *car* or *truck*
- **a subordinate level** for particular varieties of specific things – *a Jersey potato* is a kind of potato and a *Toyota Camry* is a kind of car

Here are some examples of how this works:

Superordinate level	Basic Level	Subordinate level
fruit	apple	Cox's Orange Pippin
	peach	cling peach
	orange	Seville orange
tools	hammer	claw hammer
	saw	fretsaw
	screwdriver	Phillips screwdriver
fish	salmon	wild salmon
	trout	rainbow trout
	herring	smoked herring
meat	lamb	lamb cutlet
	beef	rump steak
	pork	pork chop
reading matter	books	novels
	newspapers	*Sun*
	letters	business letters

We automatically organize what we see at the basic level. Look around the room and you will notice basic-level *chairs*, *tables*, etc. rather than superordinate *furniture* or subordinate *office chairs*. The human mind sees certain objects and shapes that it treats as basic; we see an *apple*, a *peach*, and so on. To some extent this depends on our special interests. Rosch found that while a plane's *wing* was a basic object for most of those she tested, it was a superordinate term for aircraft mechanics with many basic-level terms.

Children learn basic-level words before they learn the other levels. They start by saying *dog*, not *animal* or *Dobermann–Pinscher*. What they see around them is organized into basic levels. This is partly the consequence of how their parents present basic words to them, rather than superordinates or subordinates: "*Look! A cat!*" rather than "*Wow! An animal! A Siamese!*"

22. Proper Names to Words

Several common (and many uncommon) English words come from people's names. Sometimes a word celebrates the person who discovered something, like the Salmon in *salmonella*; sometimes the person who did something first, like the Earl of Sandwich in *sandwich*; or had a particular characteristic like Warden Spooner in *spoonerism*. Garments have been named after the great: like *cardigan* after the Earl of Cardigan; *wellington boot* after the Duke of Wellington. Plants have had *-ia* added to the name of their discoverer: as in *forsythia* from *Forsyth*; or are called after a local celebrity, as in *buddleia* from Buddle.

aubretia: Claude Aubriet, French flower painter in the eighteenth century

begonia: Michel Bégon, a governor of the French West Indies in the seventeenth century

biro: László Biró, the Hungarian who invented the ballpoint pen in the 1930s

bowdlerize: Thomas Bowdler, who in 1818 censored Shakespeare to make it acceptable for families. "Out damned spot" became "Out crimson spot," for example.

boycott: Captain Charles Boycott, an estate manager in Ireland, whose workers refused to deal with him in the late eighteenth century

buddleia: Adam Buddle (1662–1715), a botanist from Essex

cardigan: the Earl of Cardigan, who may have worn a similar garment while leading the Charge of the Light Brigade, mid-nineteenth century

clarkia: William Clark, an American explorer who co-led the first American expedition to the Pacific in 1803–6

dieldrin: Otto Diels, a Nobel Prize-winning German chemist in the twentieth century

forsythia: William Forsyth, the botanist who brought the plant back to England in 1844

fuchsia: Leonhard Fuchs, a German physician and botanist in the sixteenth century

gerrymander: Elbridge Gerry, Governor of Massachusetts, plus the *-mander* from *salamander*, said to come from the shape of his suggested electoral boundaries on the map in the late nineteenth century

guillotine: Joseph-Ignace Guillotin, who took part in the French Revolution in the late eighteenth century

hoover: the Hoover Company, which first put vacuum cleaners on sale in the U.S. in the early twentieth century

loganberry: J. H. Logan, a Californian plant breeder who crossed a raspberry and a blackberry in about 1881

lynch: Captain William Lynch, who organized lynch trials in Virginia in 1776

macadam: John Loudon Macadam, an engineer and inventor of the road surface, early nineteenth century

mackintosh: Charles Macintosh, the inventor of the process of waterproofing fabrics in the nineteenth century

maverick: Samuel Augustus Maverick (1803–70) owned cattle in Texas, which he refused to brand

pasteurize: Louis Pasteur, the inventor of the pasteurisation process to kill bacteria in liquids such as milk in the nineteenth century

sadist: Marquis de Sade, a French aristocrat who led a scandalous life in the eighteenth century

salmonella: Daniel Salmon, a U.S. administrator in charge of the research project that isolated the bacteria in the late nineteenth century

sandwich: John Montagu, the 4th Earl of Sandwich, didn't want to interrupt his gambling by pausing for dinner, so he ate meat between slices of bread, eighteenth century

saxophone: Adolphe Sax, the German inventor of the family of instruments in the nineteenth century

shrapnel: General Henry Shrapnel, an English inventor of a new type of artillery shell in the early nineteenth century

spoonerism: Reverend William Archibald Spooner, Warden of New College, Oxford, who used them spontaneously, twentieth century (see page 118)

waldo: Waldo Jones, the fictional genius in Robert Heinlein's science fiction story of the same name, 1942, who invented remote handling by suitable gloves (waldos) as he was only able to function in low gravity on board a satellite because of his physical disability

wellington boots: the 1st Duke of Wellington wore high boots in the nineteenth century

wisteria: Caspar Wistar, a nineteenth-century American anatomist

volt: Alessandro Volta (1745–1827), the Italian physicist who invented the electric battery

23. The Shortest Word

What are the shortest words in English? Obviously those that have a single sound when spoken and a single letter when written: *a, i,* and *o* ("*O Solitude,*" a song title).

Some letter names act as one-letter written words, but usually with more than one sound when spoken, *his mark was a B*, or as abbreviations like *B&B* and *32k*, or in certain expressions, *That's him to a T, Mind your p's and q's, the three Rs*. However, apart from the vowels "a, e, i, o, u," and "r," letter names in English have two or more sounds (b = bee, j = jay, etc.), so they do not count as spoken words with single sounds. A trick of text-messaging is to have "u, c, r, y" act as abbreviated words: *Y r u going 2 c him?*

24. JetSpeak
WHAT'S THE POINT OF LONG WORDS?

Announcements heard over loudspeakers in airports and planes have their own characteristics, exemplified in Jay Leno's joke that, during a flight, President Clinton had to *return the attendant to her full upright and locked position.* Here are some recent everyday specimens, collected on my weekly commuting trip between Colchester and Newcastle.

This delay is due to the late arrival of the inbound aircraft.
Does this really mean what it appears to mean: "This plane is late because it's late?"

This flight is now available for priority boarding at gate 88.
Simple English translation: "If you have paid extra, you can now board." Why say *available for boarding* rather than *you can board*?

Passengers who have purchased priority boarding are now invited to board through gate 88.
A variation on the last one, notable for *purchased* rather than *bought* and for *invited* rather than *asked* or *requested*. How exciting to be invited to something!

Would any passengers still wishing to travel on this flight please go to gate 88, where the aircraft awaits its on-time departure.
Simple English translation: "You lot in the bar, get a move on." But there's a strange overtone to the idea of *passengers wishing to travel* rather than passengers having tickets and planes waiting expectantly to leave; I have a compulsion to go to the gate and say, "Yes please, I know I'm booked to Newcastle, but I'd love to fly to Rio."

In the unlikely event of having to use a slide, please leave your carry-on baggage on board.
Simple English translation: "If you have to use a slide, don't take your bag with you." The implication of *In the unlikely event of* is "Don't worry, it may never happen," but that's pretty cumbersome. What's wrong with *if*?

We do have a non-smoking policy onboard and we would like to thank you in advance for observing this.
Simple English translation: "Don't smoke, as it's illegal." Why should we be thanked for obeying the law of the land? *Thank you in advance for not driving on the sidewalk?*

We are commencing our final descent into Stansted.
Simple English translation: "We will start descending soon." Why *commence* rather than *start*?

Written safety instructions are equally idiosyncratic.

FASTEN SEAT BELT WHILST SEATED
"Don't put your seat belt on if you're standing up?" Presumably this means "Keep your belt on all the time in your seat," but *fasten* is a one-off event, *keep on* is a continuous one. Buses have similar motifs:

PLEASE REFRAIN FROM SMOKING ON THIS VEHICLE
Why not "No smoking?" Why *refrain* and *vehicle*? All the passengers know it's a bus.

Doubtless there are technical or legal reasons for the exact wording of some announcements; they have to give a reason for the delay but don't want to admit that the engine fell off the plane you were supposed to be on. The pilots are usually much more informative about reasons for delay, such as, on one occasion, food poisoning in the crew that was supposed to be on the flight.

The underlying reason why announcements and notices have these odd forms is that organizations want to sound ultra-respectable. Given the choice between a short word like *start* and a longer word like *commence*, they choose the longer one; given a choice between a simple expression like *if* and a complex form like *in the event of*, they prefer the complex. It's a matter of elevating their language to a more upper-class, formal form.

Are they right or wrong? Many passengers doubtless expect this extra level of formality from airlines; it reassures them that the airline is responsible and respectable. Take a deviant announcement like one I once heard: *If you smoke in the toilets, we will open the back door of the plane and throw you out.* This may sound flippant and unprofessional, even if rather more direct.

While the quaintness of jetspeak is easy to poke fun at, it can be dangerous if it results in passengers not understanding the safety regulations, particularly those who are not native speakers of English. You need a higher level of English vocabulary to understand *commence*, *illuminate*, *brace*, and *whilst* and to follow the construction *in the event of* rather than *if*.

In England, the Plain English Campaign has been exhorting organizations to use clear English in official documents and forms for many years. They advise "Keep your sentences short," "Prefer short words," and "Prefer active verbs," all typical advice in style manuals for a hundred years. The Plain English Campaign provides a list of words to avoid and suggests what to put in their place: for example, use *before* rather than *prior to*, *keep to* rather than *comply with* and *end* rather than *terminate*. In a random sample of their list, the undesirable words have on average 3.8 syllables, the preferred words 1.7. Often the preferred form has a preposition: for example, *speed up* rather than *accelerate*, *find out* rather than *ascertain*.

The distinction between short and long words reflects the

different historical strata in the English vocabulary. Words that come from Old English, before the Norman Conquest, tend to be short: *buy, start*. Those that come from French or Latin tend to be longer: *purchase, commence*. The legacy of the Norman occupation is that the longer words seem higher-status or more educated, as they were associated with the language spoken by the elite rulers, French, or the language spoken by the learned, Latin.

If longer words still have this association for today's speakers of English, why should we object to it in announcements? People being thanked in advance for observing a non-smoking policy may appreciate its pompous tone more than the informal *Don't smoke*. There's no intrinsic reason to choose between *purchase* or *buy* apart from a prejudice for or against long words – provided, of course, that there is no difference in meaning between the short word and the long. In some of the Plain English examples, one word cannot be substituted for another because they mean slightly different things. Is *accelerate* (*OED*, to "quicken," i.e. increase speed continuously) really the same as the Plain English-endorsed *speed up* (*OED*, "increasing the speed or working rate of a thing," i.e. to get to a faster rate of speed)? Is *conclusion* (*OED*, "final result, upshot") quite the same as the preferred *end* (*OED*, "One of the two extremities of a line")? Because of the many meanings and overtones that go with a word, substituting a shorter word for a longer word or vice versa can change the meaning in many ways. According to the science fiction writer Theodore Sturgeon, "There are no synonyms. There are no two words that mean exactly the same thing," a sentiment that most linguists agree with.

Indeed, for the airline passenger who is not a native speaker of English some of the longer words may be easier to understand precisely because of their links to Latin and Romance languages. The meaning of *commence* should be easy to work out for a French speaker who knows *commencer*, a Spanish speaker who knows *comenzar*, or an Italian who knows *cominciare*, all derived from Latin, compared with the opaque word *start*, descended from Old English.

The use of long latinate words has, then, split people for hundreds of years. Some think them erudite and profound, while others see them as pretentious, unnecessary, and comic. Part of the Arts and Crafts movement in late-nineteenth century England was a return to the roots of English. The most radical advocate was the Dorset dialect poet William Barnes, whose overall principle was to rid English of words that did not come from Old English. Here is a sample of his numerous inventions:

botany > wortlore   ignorant > loreless
century > yearhundred   music > gleecraft
exit > outgate   omnibus > folkwain
grammar > speechcraft   photograph > sun-print

His version of "A prophet is not without honor, save in his own country" was "A foresayer is not unworthy, out-taken in his land."

25. Divided by the Atlantic
AMERICAN AND BRITISH WORDS

Most differences between everyday British English and American English are familiar and obvious. How easily can you spot whether the speaker of each of the sentences below is English or American? Answers on page 280.

	US	UK
1. The corpse was put in the boot.	☐	☐
2. Ginger, you're barmy.	☐	☐
3. The dog was digging in the dirt.	☐	☐
4. The room contained a large credenza.	☐	☐
5. My car's muffler was faulty.	☐	☐
6. The man was sitting in the bleachers.	☐	☐
7. She received a letter in the post.	☐	☐
8. The baby was wearing only a diaper.	☐	☐
9. I called him on my mobile.	☐	☐
10. She was busking in the street.	☐	☐
11. The pylon towered above the house.	☐	☐
12. They were mowing their yard.	☐	☐
13. I had grits for breakfast.	☐	☐
14. Under his shirt, he wore a dirty vest.	☐	☐
15. This place sells the cheapest gas.	☐	☐
16. My wife is visiting Paris in the fall.	☐	☐
17. I've lost the pants from this suit.	☐	☐
18. The rocket salad was very tasty.	☐	☐
19. The baby had a dummy in its mouth.	☐	☐
20. They pushed him in on a gurney.	☐	☐

Different words for (approximately) the same meaning (British one first):

autumn/fall	exhaust/muffler
boot/trunk (of car)	flannel/washcloth
braces/suspenders	mobile/cellphone
detective story/mystery	nappy/diaper
dummy/pacifier	rocket/arugula
earth/dirt	rubbish/trash or garbage
elevator/lift	terrace/bleachers
er/uh (hesitation noise)	torch/flashlight

Same word, different meaning
biscuit (a hard baked product/bread dough cooked in a frying pan)
chips (stick-like fried potatoes/crisp, i.e. thinly sliced potatoes)
diner (person who dines/café)
dirt (filth/earth)
duster (cloth for dusting/long cloak or coat)
fag (cigarette/gay)
gas (vapor such as air/petrol)
gravy (meat-based sauce/flour and milk-based sauce)
hood (headware/bonnet of a car)
muffin (small flat cake eaten hot/cake in a small cup shape)
pants (underwear/trousers)
pavement (side of road/roadway)
post (mail/pole)
vest (underwear/waistcoat)
wrapper (covering for a book/dressing gown)
yard (enclosed space/garden)

Words more or less unique to one variety
UK: barmy   busk   pylon (for electricity)
US: arugula   bleachers   credenza   grits   gurney   pacifier

Words where the actual animal is different in North America and Europe
blackbird   hare   rabbit   squirrel

Do these differences really cause communication problems? Many American terms are now familiar to British people through novels, film and television. A British academic teaching in the States who was trying to clean the blackboard asked his class if they knew where the rubber was, to the consternation of his students – *rubber* means "eraser" in England, "condom" in the U.S. Defending herself against a murder charge in the States, a British nanny said she *popped him on the bed*. According to the prosecution, this was an admission of guilt, as *pop* means "kill" in the U.S.; however, as the defense pointed out, *pop* means "place" in informal use in England.

One undoubted source of confusion is the difference between the British meaning of *first floor* as "the floor above the ground floor" and the American meaning of "first floor" (synonymous with "ground floor"). It is easy enough to work out which is the first floor in England or the U.S. But what if the receptionist in a hotel in Canada, Singapore, or Dubai tells you your room is on the first floor? Particularly when the recorded voice in the elevator uses a counting system different from the receptionist's.

26. Indian Words in English

Ever since the British went to India, many words from Indian languages have traveled in the reverse direction. The changing historical relationship between the two countries is shown in the different kinds of words that the English language borrowed at different periods, according to the Indian expert Subba Roa.

- In the seventeenth century it was trade that counted. The names of Indian places were used for particular materials, such as *calico* (a city) or *cashmere* (Kashmir).
- In the eighteenth century, though trade continued to bring in words such as *jute* and *seersucker*, influences came from Indian culture, such as *hookah* (a smoking device), and the military, as in *sepoy* (native Indian soldier).
- The nineteenth century saw Indian words used with wider meanings than in their original languages, *jungle* (just "waste ground"), *toddy* ("tree sap"), and *juggernaut* ("wagon"), while ideas from Indian philosophy began to be known, such as *karma*.
- The twentieth century continued the military influence, with the two world wars yielding *Blighty* and *cushy*.

Here are some other words that seem to have come from India, a matter not just of recognizable imports like *tikka massala*, but also of *bungalow* and *loot*.

atoll, Malayalam "closing, uniting"
bandanna, Hindustani "a method of dyeing"
basmati, Hindi "fragrant"
bungalow, Hindustani "belonging to Bengal"
calico, Malayalam "city name"
catamaran, Tamil "tied tree"

chintz, Sanskrit "variegated"
dinghy, Hindi "small boat"
dungaree, Hindi "coarse calico"
guru, Hindi/Hindustani "a teacher, priest"
gymkhana, Hindustani "ball-house"
khaki, Urdu/Persian "dust-colored"
loot, Hindi "booty"
mantra, Sanskrit "a thought"
mulligatawny, Tamil "black pepper"
pukka, Punjabi "cooked, mature"
pundit, Hindi "learned man"
shampoo, Hindi, "to press/massage"
teak, Tamil "teak tree"
thug, Hindi "a cheat"
tom-tom, Hindustani "drum"
veranda, Bengali "porch"

27. Written Words That are Seldom Spoken

The written language of notices often uses words that are extremely rare, if not obsolete, in spoken language. My favorite in England is *Do not park on the greensward*, which makes one think of Robin Hood driving an SUV.

Here are some current notices using words that are hardly ever spoken:

MAIN ENTRANCE CLOSED.
PLEASE USE ALTERNATE MEANS OF ENTRY/EGRESS
I have never heard *egress* in speech, perhaps because it is regional. Yet the notice expects me to know it means "exit" in written English. Doubtless there are *EMERGENCY EGRESS* signs in buildings, to the bewilderment of many.

BEFORE BOARDING LET PEOPLE ALIGHT FIRST
Apart from some train announcements, do you ever hear anyone say *alight*? Nevertheless it is common enough in written notices: for example, on the Newcastle Metro.

VEHICULAR ACCESS
Surely no one but a bureaucrat would say *vehicular*.

LIFE-JACKET DONNING INSTRUCTIONS
King Arthur may have donned his armor; most of us put our jackets on.

NO DOG FOULING
We mustn't foul dogs in public? Dogs mustn't foul people? Can you imagine someone saying *Don't foul my armchair*?

There is a contradiction between the needs of the public to understand such notices and the way that they are expressed in writing. Presumably their writers feel they need to assert the power of the relevant authority through pompous written language. One giveaway is the overuse of capital letters to show importance. If they actually wanted to make their notices usable, they would combine capitals with lower-case characters, which are far more legible than capitals by themselves.

One notice that balances safety with the demands of authority was placed on a pole several feet out in a lake at the University of Essex: OUT OF BOUNDS.

The campus was the location for summer schools for hundreds of Italian schoolchildren. How likely were they to know such vocabulary, familiar to most of us only from our time at school, where areas were decreed *out of bounds*? Needless to say, a few yards from this notice was another proclaiming: CYCLISTS MUST DISMOUNT.

Turning to another form of public notice, an area rich in written words that are more or less dead in spoken language but are used in signs, is shops: *haberdasher, confectioner, hosier, ironmonger, cheesemonger* … I never say, *Do you know a good haberdasher?* or *I need to buy some hardware and confectionery*, but there may be people who still do – some words may reenter the spoken language from written signs. Most of us have a spoken form with *-shop* – *sweetshop, clothes shop*, and so on – and would think someone was trying to be strange if they said *I know a good hosier*. Regional variants include *fleshers* and *ice-cream parlors*. Shops seek a fake antiquity by calling themselves *apothecaries*. Again the overriding motive is to lay claim to the virtues of age by using written forms that we seldom if ever say.

28. Sex and Gender

In languages like French and German every word has a grammatical gender even if it does not have a sex: for example, *sedia*, "chair," is feminine in Italian, while in German *Ball*, "ball," is masculine and famously *Mädchen*, "girl," is neuter.

In English words, gender is fairly unobtrusive as it affects only pronouns *he/she/it* according to "natural" gender. Words referring to the male sex go with the masculine gender, *man > he*, those referring to the female sex with the feminine, *woman > she*, and those referring to things with no relevant sex with the neuter gender, *house > it*.

There are nevertheless complications:

- some words go with either feminine or masculine pronouns, depending on who is being talked about: *doctor > he/she*, etc.
- some words are linked to gender by their form, such as the feminine *-ess* and *-ette* endings, which are dying out: *actress, mistress, usherette, majorette*.
- some words vary in gender. Parents are unlikely to use *it* about their own baby, unlike strangers. Ships and cars can be *it* or *she*, depending on one's enthusiasm for them. The moon is normally *it* but *she* poetically.
- "higher" animals have genders: *bull > he / cow > she*; "lower" creatures do not: *ant > it*.
- countries can have gender pronouns: *France in all her glory*; but not for sports: *France is using its best team*.

Other languages have "arbitrary gender," meaning that the gender distinction is a grammatical quirk rather than directly linked to sex. A toothbrush is the masculine *spazzolino* in Italian, the feminine *Zahnburste* in German. Studies across languages have found few overlaps in the gender that is assigned to objects.

See if you can guess the gender of these words. Answers are on page 280.

Italian	M	F	German	M	F
1. *materasso*, "mattress"	☐	☐	6. *Uhr*, "clock"	☐	☐
2. *matita*, "pencil"	☐	☐	7. *Schublade*, "drawer"	☐	☐
3. *poltrona*, "armchair"	☐	☐	8. *Strohhalm*, "straw"	☐	☐
4. *violino*, "violin"	☐	☐	9. *Stecker*, "plug"	☐	☐
5. *chiave*, "key"	☐	☐	10. *Zeitung*, "newspaper"	☐	☐

The effects of linguistic gender on our thinking have fascinated researchers in recent years. Children struggle to find the link between the gender of nouns and the sex of objects in the world. An advertising campaign for sportswear featured a talking football. In Portuguese it had a woman's voice, in German a man's voice, reflecting the different gender of the word for football in the two languages. While feminists who speak English managed to get words like *chairman* replaced by *chair* or *chairperson*, where do you begin in a language where feminine includes chairs (French), air (German) and pizza (Italian)?

29. Where in the World Do They Come From?

REGIONAL ENGLISHES

This list tests how well you recognize the varieties of English spoken in different parts of the world. Check the box on the opposite page for the regional type of English you associate with each word. Answers on page 281.

Whether these are really regional can be tested on the website *Which Language Variety?*, www.pojkfilmsklubben.org/cgi-bin/langtools/whichVariety.cgi. This shows how often a word occurs on webpages with email addresses for particular regions: .uk, .ca, etc. The word *drongo*, for instance, is 79 percent Australian and New Zealand addresses, 20 percent UK; *busk* is 55 percent UK and Ireland, 37 percent Australia and New Zealand, 7 percent Canada and U.S.; *bleachers* is 95.6 percent U.S. and Canada, 4 percent UK and Ireland.

One snag with this method is that Internet addresses do not specify U.S. addresses, so the website has to use addresses with .com that are obviously in the U.S., like: latimes.com. Another snag is that it has not been extended to India, Singapore, etc. Nevertheless it does produce some surprises. Why, for example, is *chummie* so Canadian at 37 percent with everywhere else in the low twenties? Why is *bloke* 67 percent in Australia and New Zealand, 29 percent in the UK and Ireland, and almost unknown elsewhere?

	Australia/NZ	India	Singapore	South Africa	UK/Ireland	US/Canada
1. daggy (awkward, nerdish)	☐	☐	☐	☐	☐	☐
2. lekker (nice)	☐	☐	☐	☐	☐	☐
3. razoo (I haven't a brass razoo = coin)	☐	☐	☐	☐	☐	☐
4. rutabaga (swede)	☐	☐	☐	☐	☐	☐
5. yakka (hard work)	☐	☐	☐	☐	☐	☐
6. pukka (real)	☐	☐	☐	☐	☐	☐
7. atas (snob)	☐	☐	☐	☐	☐	☐
8. undershirt (vest)	☐	☐	☐	☐	☐	☐
9. kiff (nice, great etc.)	☐	☐	☐	☐	☐	☐
10. toot (stupid)	☐	☐	☐	☐	☐	☐
11. opticals (spectacles)	☐	☐	☐	☐	☐	☐
12. airdash (air travel)	☐	☐	☐	☐	☐	☐
13. prepone (opposite of postpone)	☐	☐	☐	☐	☐	☐
14. kopi (coffee)	☐	☐	☐	☐	☐	☐
15. backie (pickup truck)	☐	☐	☐	☐	☐	☐
16. candy floss (spun-sugar sweet)	☐	☐	☐	☐	☐	☐
17. yaar (friend)	☐	☐	☐	☐	☐	☐
18. ladybug (ladybird)	☐	☐	☐	☐	☐	☐
19. maha (great)	☐	☐	☐	☐	☐	☐
20. bludger (lazy person)	☐	☐	☐	☐	☐	☐
21. chop (to stamp)	☐	☐	☐	☐	☐	☐
22. rowhouse (terrace house)	☐	☐	☐	☐	☐	☐
23. skive (abscond from work/school)	☐	☐	☐	☐	☐	☐
24. 'cher (teacher)	☐	☐	☐	☐	☐	☐
25. roundabout (traffic circle)	☐	☐	☐	☐	☐	☐
26. tinny (can of beer)	☐	☐	☐	☐	☐	☐
27. gogo (grandma/elderly woman)	☐	☐	☐	☐	☐	☐
28. pushchair (baby buggy)	☐	☐	☐	☐	☐	☐
29. garbage (rubbish)	☐	☐	☐	☐	☐	☐
30. skollie (gangster)	☐	☐	☐	☐	☐	☐

30. Atoms of Meaning

Do words have meanings as wholes? In this case each word would be quite different from every other word: the word *man* would mean something quite different from the word *woman* or the word *person*.

Or does the meaning of a word consist of basic elements which it shares with other words, rather like splitting a molecule up into basic elements such as electrons and quarks? An example is the meanings of words for people, say *girl* and *boy*. The difference between them consists of a meaning feature [male/female]. So *boy* is [+male], *girl* [+female]. This can of course be phrased in either way by saying that *girl* is [–male] or *boy* is [–female]; neither alternative would please everybody. Suppose we now add in a contrast of age – *man* and *woman*. This needs an extra feature [± mature]:

man	+male –female +mature
boy	+male –female –mature
woman	–male +female +mature
girl	–male +female –mature

What about other words? Take *mother* and *father*. This pair adds a further feature [± parent]:

father	+male +mature +parent
mother	+female +mature +parent

Or we can go to other species:

bull	+male +mature
calf	–mature
bitch	+female
tadpole	–mature

Crucial elements of meaning are shared among many words, such as gender [±male/female] and age [±mature]. This does not mean that these elements are necessarily present in all words; the word *calf* does not include an element for gender, any more than the word *baby* or *child*, even if all three share the element [–mature].

This approach can be extended to other areas of meaning. Take *drinks*, which all share an element [+liquid] compared to, say, *food* [–liquid]. *Tea* is normally hot [+hot] and non-alcoholic [–alcohol]; if we want iced tea or tea with a shot of gin, we'd have to specify it in addition to the word itself.

tea   +liquid +hot –alcohol

Lemonade and *cola*, on the other hand, are normally served cold:

cola   +liquid –hot –alcohol
lemonade   +liquid –hot –alcohol

Beer is also served cold (even if the exact temperature varies) and it is alcoholic, as is *whisky*. You can ask for *a hot whiskey* in Dublin, but again you always need to specify when the meaning goes against the normal features of the word:

beer   +liquid –hot +alcohol
whisky   +liquid –hot +alcohol

And, if you're a serious drinker of whisky, you can soon add meaning elements of [±Scotch], [±single malt], [±Lowland] [±Island], etc. ending up with all the meanings of specific Scotches like Laphroaig or Glenmorangie.

These elements of meaning have played an important role in the discussion of discrimination in language for many years. Is a *chairman* necessarily [+male] or can a woman be a chairman?

There are certainly precedents for [+female] *mayors* and [+male] *mayoresses* (the mayor's consort regardless of sex).

The feature of age can be equally inflammatory. Calling a [+mature] man a [−mature] *boy* is extremely rude. Does the same apply to calling a [+mature] woman a [−mature] *girl*? Thirty years ago *girl* was held to be as insulting as *boy*. But now it seems the pendulum is swinging back. *Girl* can suggest youth and is increasingly used by [+mature] young women about themselves. Think of pop groups like the *Spice Girls*, *Girls Aloud* and *Wonder Girls*; *Sugababes* perhaps takes the [−mature] meaning to its logical ultimate.

The features view of meanings also affects children's learning of words. At one stage children know that *big* and *small* have a meaning to do with size, but they do not know the component [±large] so they get confused between them and seem to choose randomly which word is big and which small. The same happens to *before* and *after*: they know that these are something to do with time but have no element [±prior] to tell them which comes first. Other pairs that have been studied include *deep/shallow*, *tall/short*, and *more/less*, all of which are confused by children at this stage.

A deceptive aspect of children's language acquisition of words is that they often appear to use a word perfectly when they actually lack some vital feature. They have a partial grasp of what the word means. A familiar example is the early use of *daddy* to apply to any male stranger; children have learnt that *daddy* is [+male] but not that it is [+my parent]. My son once said, *I have a headache in my stomach*. Clearly he had learned that *headache* has a feature [+pain] but not that it is marked as [+in the head].

Those who are learning a second language have much the same problem. They know a word but they do not know all the features of its meaning. Learners of Samoan confuse *umi* (long) with *puupuu* (short) because they have acquired the feature [+length] but not the feature [±greater]. Nevertheless, this features analysis works only for a small part of the English vocabulary and is just one of the processes in children's acquisition of words.

Here's a list of famous people. Try to work out a set of meaning features that would distinguish all the words on the list. You can test how successful you are by reading out the list to someone and seeing if they can guess who you are describing – a version of the game of *Twenty Questions*.

Word	Feature 1	Feature 2	Feature 3	Feature 4
1. Meryl Streep	....	....	....	....
2. Queen Elizabeth I	....	....	....	....
3. Barack Obama	....	....	....	....
4. Lewis Hamilton	....	....	....	....
5. Lady Macbeth	....	....	....	....
6. Mick Jagger	....	....	....	....
7. David Cameron	....	....	....	....
8. Lisa Simpson	....	....	....	....
9. Britney Spears	....	....	....	....
10. George Clooney	....	....	....	....

31. Word Games with Letter Arrangement

The word games in this book are for more than one person rather than the sorts of puzzle that are normally done by individuals, which are available in many books.

One type of word game involves forming a word out of an arbitrary collection of letters, as in the commercially available *Scrabble*, *Kanugo*, and *Lexicon*. Skill is a matter of finding the combination that makes a word with the maximum possible score, i.e. getting the Q on a triple-letter square in Scrabble, and of knowing the frequencies of letters in the Scrabble set of a hundred tiles – twelve E's, six T's, one Q, etc., similar to but not quite the same as the frequency list for English as a whole. This usually relies on an arbitrary set of words, such as those in an established dictionary, rather than everyday English vocabulary. Books on Scrabble include such two-letter words as *aa*, *bo*, *ka*, *ky*, *od*, *qi*, *ri*, *xi* and *ut*. A less familiar variant is *Up Words*, where players pile letter cards on top of other letters so the words are never fixed as they are in Scrabble.

But all of these are essentially playing with surface features of words, i.e. the letters and their sequence, not with the essence of the word – its meaning. Does anybody care what *aa* means? (In fact, the *OED* has two entries for *aa*, one obsolete meaning "stream," one current meaning "a rough, scoriaceous lava.") The numbers of *Sudoku* have as much connection with our knowledge of English as the arbitrary words of competition Scrabble.

Pen-and-paper letter arrangement games usually require at least a knowledge of English spelling. *Ghosts* was a favorite of James Thurber. In this, one person chooses a word without telling anyone else and announces the first letter, say *b* for *British*. The next player has to continue spelling a possible word and adds *a* to get *ba* for *battle*. And so on. The trick is that the player must not finish the word, once it has passed three letters in length. Players may be challenged to test if they are thinking of a real English word. Lives are lost when words are finished and when challenges are failed; three lives gone and you're a ghost. In a challenging version known as *Superghosts*, letters may be added at the end, in the middle, or at the beginning of the word.

32. Stuff and Nonsense
PHRASES WITH "AND"

Some words are often found together in pairs and trios and so on, technically know as "collocations." One kind consists of two words joined with an *and*. Complete the following pairs with *and*. Answers are on page 283.

black and ....

body and ....

bread and ....

come and ....

foot and ....

give and ....

health and ....

here and ....

hook and ....

hue and ....

huffed and ....

in and ....

kiss and ....

kith and ....

Laurel and ....

now and ....

off and ....

on and ....

open and ....

over and ....

part and ....

pins and ....

round and ....

skin and ....

son and ....

the quick and the ....

time and ....

to and ....

touch and ....

town and ....

These *and* combinations are so predictable and common we take them for granted. They illustrate another way in which English phrases have meanings that are distinct from the words taken separately: *black* by itself and *blue* by itself do not add up to the phrase *black and blue*, meaning "badly bruised," even if sometimes they can be used literally, *the magazine cover is black and blue*. The meaning of *pins and needles* cannot be worked out by adding *pins* to *needles*. You can of course combine almost any two meanings with *and* to get a new phrase, but it won't mean more than the sum of its two parts, as we see when we change the vocabulary of familiar phrases.

| hue and fly | pins and scissors | touch and see |
| huffed and stuffed | skin and hide | black and pink |

Some *and* phrases repeat a word with more or less the same meaning in a semi-rhyming way: *kith and kin, huffed and puffed, time and tide*. Sometimes the words have a close meaning relationship: *bread and butter* or *skin and bone*. At other times they are opposites: *off and on, in sickness and in health*, or *thick and thin*. Many show the two-beat stress pattern common since Old English, found for instance in titles of books and films: <u>War</u> and <u>Peace</u>, *The* <u>Dark</u> <u>Knight</u>, <u>Gone</u> with the <u>Wind</u>, <u>Mamma</u> <u>Mia</u>, etc.

Research by vocabulary experts Dongkwang Shin and Paul Nation has shown that overall the top ten collocations in English are: *you know, I think, a bit, always used to, as well, a lot of* (noun), (number) *pounds, thank you*, (number) *years, in fact*.

33. Body Parts in Metaphors

The metaphors we use every day often refer to the different parts of the body. Here is a quick check on some of these. Answers on page 283.

1. Which part of the body do you bury in something? ....
2. Which part of the body are you tied by? ....
3. Which part of the body do you pull out? ....
4. Which part of the body do you give someone? ....
5. Which part of another person's body can you be under?

   ....
6. Which part of another person's body do you pull? ....
7. Which part of another person's body do you weep on?

   ....
8. Which part of another person's body do you breathe down?

   ....
9. Which part of the body do you twist? ....
10. Which part of the body do you shake? ....
11. Which part of the body do you pay through? ....
12. Which part of another person's body do you fall upon?

    ....
13. Which part of the body do you speak through? ....
14. Which part(s) of the body do you give? ....
15. Which part of the body do you cool? ....
16. Which part of the body do you put down? ....
17. Which part of the body do you have in the clouds? ....
18. Which part of the body do you keep to the ground? ....

Arms

I'd give an arm and a leg/my
   right arm
The strong/long arm of the law
You'd have to twist my arm
At arm's length
Greet with open arms

Legs

Show your legs/leg it
Pull your leg
On your last legs
Shake a leg

Hands

Get a big hand
A safe pair of hands
Live hand to mouth
Win hands down
Give your hand

Feet

Land feet first
Stand on your own two feet
Put your foot down
Catch on the wrong foot
Get your foot in the door

Neck

Get it in the neck
Breathe down someone's neck
Neck-and-neck
Neck of the woods

Nose

Nose in the air
See beyond one's nose
Pay through the nose
Keep your nose clean
Bury one's nose in

Head

Two heads are better than one
Have your head in the clouds
Keep your head above water
Do it standing on your head

Much English vocabulary consists of such phrases. You don't know English until you know that you put your foot, not your fist down, you get it in the neck, not the stomach, and shaking a leg is not the same as shaking a hand.

34. English Names for Foreign Places

Often the English name of a foreign place bears slight resemblance to anything its inhabitants would say. Sometimes this is simply due to differences in pronunciation or spelling, for example *Brussels* versus *Bruxelles*. Recently places' names have been respelled to bring the English pronunciation more in line with that of the inhabitants, for instance *Peking* becoming *Beijing* or *Canton* becoming *Guangdong*. Or it may show independence of their Western-created name, *Formosa* (from Portuguese) becoming *Taiwan*, *Ceylon* (English from Portuguese) becoming *Sri Lanka* (from Sanskrit), or *Rhodesia* (from Cecil Rhodes) becoming *Zimbabwe*. The English name sometimes draws on a name from an earlier period, *Germany* for *Deutschland*, based on the Latin name *Germania*, or on another language, *Padua* for Italian *Padova* seems closer to the name *Padoa* in the Venetian language than *Padova* in Italian.

English name	Name in the language of the inhabitants
Athens	Athina
Austria	Österreich
Bavaria	Bayern
Belgium	Belgique
Benares	Varanasi (renamed)
Bombay	Mumbai (renamed, but during the hotel massacre in 2008 commentators claimed the inhabitants still called it Bombay)
Brussels	Bruxelles (French), Brussel (Dutch)
Burma	Myanmar (renamed)
Calcutta	Kolkata (renamed)
China	Zhōnghuá (English form based on Qin, a particular ruling dynasty)
Cologne	Köln (Colonia Agrippina in Latin)

Copenhagen	København (English form from Low German)
Davos	Pronounced by the media as "<u>dah</u>voss," by the inhabitants as "der<u>vohs</u>"
Elsinore	Helsingör
Florence	Firenze (Florentia in Latin)
Geneva	Genf (German), Genève (French), Ginevra (Italian)
Genoa	Genova
Germany	Deutschland (Germania in Latin)
Ghent	Gent (in Dutch), Gand (in French)
Greece	Ellás
The Hague	Den Haag
Holland	Nederland (the Netherlands; Holland is in fact only a region of the country)
Hungary	Magyarország (Hungaria in medieval Latin)
Japan	Nippon (Land of the Rising Sun)
Lake Geneva	Lac Leman (Lacus Lemannus in Latin)
Madras	Chennai (renamed)
Milan	Milano
Moscow	Moskva
Munich	München (the English name Munich is often pronounced with a fricative "ch" like Scottish *loch*, as if it were a German word)
Naples	Napoli
Padua	Padova (Italian), Padoa (Venetian)
Prague	Praha
Rangoon	Yangon (renamed)
Rome	Roma
Switzerland	Schweiz (German), Suisse (French), Svizzera (Italian), Svizra (Romansh), Confœderatio Helvetica (Latin on stamps, CH on number plates, etc.)
Turin	Torino
Venice	Venezia (Italian), Venezsia (Venetian)
Vienna	Wien
Wales	Cymru (Welsh)

35. Did Jeeves Speak French?

FRENCH WORDS IN ENGLISH

A high proportion of modern English words came from French, mostly being borrowed during the Middle English period from the Norman Conquest in 1066 to the late fifteenth century and the Early Modern English period to the mid-seventeenth century. Some also came in from Latin, the language of the educated classes during the same period, though often it is hard to say whether the source is Latin directly or indirectly via French. A few French borrowings like garage and police are more recent, as shown by their pronunciation – if police had been in the language long it would rhyme with nice; garage is still in transition between the French-based pronunciation rhyming with barrage and the English pronunciation rhyming with garbage. To show how much these contribute to any piece of English, here are some short samples. The French words are given in SMALL CAPS, the Latin in italics.

P. G. Wodehouse, My Man Jeeves – 1919

Jeeves – my man, you know – is REALly a most extraordinary chap. So CAPABLE. HONESTly, I shouldn't know what to do without him. On broader lines he's like those chappies who sit peering sadly over the MARBLE BATTLEMENTS at the PennSYLvania STATION in the place marked "INQUIRIES." You know the Johnnies I mean. You go up to them and say: "When's the next TRAIN for MelonsquashVILLE, Tennessee?" and they REPLY, without stopping to think, "Two-forty-three, TRACK ten, CHANGE at San Francisco." And they're right every time. Well, Jeeves gives you JUST the same IMPRESSION of omniscience.

T. S. Eliot, The Waste Land, 1922

APRIL is the CRUELLest month, breeding
LILACS out of the dead land, MIXING
MEMORY and DESIRE, stirring

Dull roots with spring rain.
Winter kept us warm, COVERING
Earth in forgetful snow, feeding
A little life with dried *tubers*.

Sayings attributed to John F. Kennedy, 1950s–1960s

It is an *unfortunate fact* that we can *secure* PEACE only by PREPARING
for WAR.

Children are the world's most VALUABLE RESOURCE and its best hope
for the FUTURE.

Mothers all want their sons to grow up to be PRESIDENT, but they don't
want them to become POLITICIANS in the PROCESS.

Forgive your ENEMIES, but never forget their names.

The fact that an English word once came from French does not
mean that it still has the same form or meaning in modern French.
The French spoken in England after 1066 was Norman French, dif-
fering in many ways from the modern Parisian variety, so that
English has the Norman *war* rather than the Parisian *guerre, cab-
bage* rather than *chou* and *garden* rather than *jardin*. Sometimes
words have come from both forms of French, leaving
us with alternatives such as *guarantee/warranty* and *guard/ward*.

36. Historian or Lawgiver?

THE PURPOSES OF DICTIONARIES

To the non-specialist, a dictionary is the ultimate source of information about words. You are allowed to use a word because it's in the dictionary. You know how to spell it and you know what it means because the dictionary tells you. You can settle an argument or win points at Scrabble by appealing to the dictionary. So I know that *regolith* means "solid material covering bedrock" because the *Oxford English Dictionary* (*OED*) tells me so. The dictionary is a judge handing down decisions about each word of the language – a wise authority interpreting the rules for a particular case. A dictionary lays down the law and tells you what you must or mustn't say.

To the language specialist, on the other hand, dictionaries are neutral descriptions of what people say and write, a referee or neutral observer, not a judge. The *OED* had the aim of including any English word that has been used since 1150. It establishes what each word meant in its original context by giving quotations to show that, say, *silly* meant something like "unsophisticated" up till the eighteenth century. Recent dictionaries emphasize the words that are in use today, not the history of words: if *iPod* or *hammered* is said, then it must be put in the dictionary. Dictionaries rapidly go out of date – *iPhone* is still not in the online *OED*, for example. The purpose of a dictionary for the linguist, contrary to popular belief, is to record what people say, not to tell them what *not* to say. It's the difference between mapping the human genome and advocating eugenics. The American writer Samuel Hayakawa summed it up: "The writer of a dictionary is a historian, not a lawgiver."

Suppose you come across *weather advisory* used as a noun and don't know what it means. You might guess it from the context – that is after all how we learn the meanings for most words –

"forecast"? Or you can go to a dictionary and discover it means "bulletin" in the USA. This is the straightforward use of a dictionary to find out the meaning of a word you haven't encountered before, more valuable in bilingual translation dictionaries because you're less likely to know a word in a second language than in your first.

Or suppose someone tells you the word you've just said, say *humungous*, is not a word at all. You look it up in the dictionary and it's not there. Oh dear, you're ashamed and will avoid it in future. But it may be the dictionary that is ignorant, not you. All dictionaries are based on a small sample of English taken from the immense amount spoken and written every day. Listen to a person talking constantly on a mobile at a rate of, say, 200 words a minute – 12,000 an hour. Think of a teacher talking for, say, five hours a day – 60,000 words, 300,000 a week, 12 million a year. Now multiply by the number of native English speakers, say 350 million, or the number of people who use English as a second language in the world, at least a billion. Despite trying to take in every word that's said, a dictionary can only be based on a minute fraction of the English spoken every minute of every day. The seven Harry Potter novels are something like 1.5 million words long, the written output of just one person. Wikipedia alone has 2.8 million entries at the time of writing, still a small fraction of the English spoken or written every day.

So it's hardly surprising that dictionaries miss some words. Perhaps your word happens to be local to your region and not visible to the dictionary makers – say *folly* in the sense of *alleyway* for the inhabitants of Colchester, England. But that's the dictionary's problem, not yours.

New words come into the language all the time, like *shockumentary* and *blog*. The lead time between the dictionary makers finding the word in a text and getting the dictionary into print can be considerable, though in principle it is shorter now that dictionaries are available in updatable electronic form. It is hard to be certain that your word is wrong simply because it's not in a dictionary; it may not have been recorded in the dictionary's sample or may have come into the language after the dictionary was compiled or be so technical that the dictionary ignores it. The practical problem is whether people understand you, not whether the word is sanctioned by some dictionary.

The debate between the specialist and the non-specialist flared up notoriously with the publication of the third edition of the American *Webster's Dictionary* in 1961. Many were shocked that this dictionary had resigned its role as judge over the English language by including words such as *ain't*, as "used orally in most parts of the U.S. by many cultivated speakers." Linguists were amazed at the public's misconception of their role of observers of language: if people say *ain't*, then it's the dictionary's duty to include it.

It is not out of the question that a dictionary should lay down the law about words. Dr. Johnson aimed in his 1755 dictionary to "preserve the purity and ascertain [make certain] the meaning of our English idiom"; the very fact that the meaning of *ascertain* has changed shows he didn't succeed. The French Academy has tried to lay down permissible words in French: for example, *ordinateur* rather than *computer*. But it's rather like King Canute proving you can't control the tide: you can catch a few words but you can't stop the sheer flood continuously rolling in.

Most modern English dictionaries are based on a corpus of English – a collection of sentences amassed from as wide and representative a range of sources as possible. Their justification is that they tell the reader the words that are being used today and what they mean, a kind of opinion poll of words, rather than reflecting the judgements and opinions of the dictionary maker. Like opinion polls, they neutrally provide the data on which other people can decide what should happen.

Of course, dictionaries have to sell themselves to purchasers. Every year dictionary publishers parade this season's fashion accessory. One makes a fuss of the new words that have been added, another of its new enormous database, both just doing their normal jobs. Another highlights its new system of including bad spellings to help bad spellers; perhaps a useful little trick but most people nowadays don't need a dictionary for this, only a spelling checker. In other words, dictionary makers have to balance their core scientific duty against their need to sell books; dictionaries are valuable properties for publishers.

37. English Words in Japanese

Many English words have been borrowed into Japanese. These are often recognizable even when they are written in the Japanese alphabetic script (*romaji*) rather than the character script (*Kanji*). The reason is the difference between Japanese and English pronunciation. Japanese syllables only have a single consonant at the beginning – "<u>ta</u>," "<u>do</u>," etc. and never end in a consonant, apart from "n." So English words borrowed into Japanese are often padded out with extra vowels to separate the consonants and to make certain that the word ends in a vowel: for example, *supana* (spanner). Japanese also makes no distinction between the sounds "r" and "l," yielding *teeburu* (table). Finally Japanese goes in for shortening long English words, as in *sekuhara* (sexual harassment). Often the meaning of a word is substantially changed. Japanese *bosu*, for instance, comes from English *boss* but means "gang leader."

Here are some common Japanese words with their English originals:

sutoraiiki: strike

sarariiman: salaryman (i.e. company worker)

suteeshon: station

nekutai: necktie

gurin-piisu: green peas

rajio: radio

sandoicchiman: sandwich man

hotto rain: hotline

taipuraita: typewriter

haado-uea: hardware

puroguraamu: program

doraggu: drugs

happii-endo: happy ending

hanbaagaa: hamburger

muudi: moody (pleasant and cozy)

waa-puro: word processor

saidaa: cider (lemonade)

famiresu: family restaurant

purintaa: printer

arubamu: photo album

kurippu: paper clip

ofisu: office

posutokaado: postcard

pasokon: personal computer

konbini: convenience store

Now see if you can guess which English words these Japanese words come from. Answers are on page 284.

1. *elebeetaa* ....
2. *hoteru* ....
3. *sakkaa* ....
4. *meron* ....
5. *biiru* ....
6. *koora* ....
7. *kurisumasu* ....
8. *hottodoggu* ....
9. *guddobai/gubbai* ....
10. *kyatto fuudo* ....

38. Word Associations

What is the first word you think of when you see the word *blue*? Most people say *sky*, *black*, *green*, *red* or *white*. However, word associations do vary considerably from one person to another. One woman's association with *blue* was *kind of*, completely baffling until she explained she had just been listening to the Miles Davis album *Kind of Blue*.

Try this out on yourself by giving the first word that comes into your head for each word in the following list. Then check whether your answers are in the top five, in order of popularity, in the list on pages 99–100.

 1. bread   ....
 2. on   ....
 3. love   ....
 4. bird   ....
 5. London   ....
 6. drive   ....
 7. drink   ....
 8. sky   ....
 9. hot   ....
10. with   ....
11. quickly   ....
12. Mozart   ....
13. Welsh   ....
14. spring   ....
15. carefully   ....
16. beer   ....

17. carrot   ....
18. plane   ....
19. television   ....
20. Chicago   ....

Look at your answers and see which of these categories they fall into.

- rhyming words: *dove* for *love*. This is a reaction to the spoken form of the word, without taking in its meaning.
- words that continue a phrase and are different parts of speech from the first word (i.e. adjective + noun rather than noun + noun): *blue sky* for *sky* (adjective + noun). To make this type of association, you have both to know the meaning and to imagine a phrase that will fit appropriately.
- words that give an alternative example from the same word type, i.e. *butter* for *bread* (noun + noun). Again this relies on knowing not only the meaning of the word but also the group of words to which it belongs and choosing something that suits the meaning.

Adults mostly give the *butter/bread* (noun + noun) type of response. They have a large stock of words to choose from, as we can see from the examples below, organized in their minds by part of speech – *sky/cloud* (noun + noun), *with/without* (preposition + preposition), *quickly/fast* (adverb + adverb).

People who don't know a language well tend to give a *blue/sky* type of response: *hot/house* (adjective + noun), *bird/fly* (noun + verb), *on/time* (preposition + noun). If you hear a new word like *squitch*, you can't very well supply a word with a similar meaning. But you can always add an adjective like *good* – *good squitch* – even if you don't know what a squitch is. These responses are therefore most common from children and from learners of English as a second language, who are also the most prone to the rhyming *dove/love*, *moon/June* response.

Words do not exist in isolation but are connected in a vast network of meanings. When we think of *drink*, it makes us think of *water*, *beer*, *thirst*, etc. As well as its literal meaning of "place," the word *London* makes us think of *city*, *bridge*, and *England*. It's as if the words in our mental dictionary are linked by invisible broadband connections that are buzzing away all the time as we speak.

Since Jung and Freud, word associations have been a familiar tool for psychologists to get at the subconscious aspects of the human mind. In the comic novel *Number Nine* by A. P. Herbert, one of the selection tasks for the British Civil Service is to get applicants to give a string of word associations. One character who is trying to fail the test deliberately associates any target word with *bottom*:

> steep > hill > down > avalanche > bottom
> mother > babies > smack > bottom
> black > bottom
> bayonet > Russians > puncture > bottoms

Another character always ends up with *bed*:

> steep > stairs > bed
> mother > baby > bed
> black > pyjamas > bed
> bayonet > wounded > bed

Most frequent associations according to Scotland's *Edinburgh Associative Thesaurus*:

1.	bread	butter, water, loaf, food, money
2.	on	off, top, in, time, to
3.	love	hate, sex, girl, life, marriage
4.	bird	fly, girl, tree, song, feathers
5.	London	city, town, bridge, home, capital
6.	drive	car, in, mad, away, carefully
7.	drink	water, beer, thirst, eat, drunk

8.	sky	blue, cloud, stars, night, high
9.	hot	cold, cool, dog, house, humid
10.	with	without, out, together, her, me
11.	quickly	fast, slowly, now, run, speed
12.	Mozart	music, piano, Beethoven, classic, concerto
13.	Welsh	rarebit, Irish, nationalist, Wales, English
14.	spring	summer, bed, time, fever, jump
15.	carefully	carelessly, slowly, care, done, gently
16.	beer	drink, drunk, froth, barrel, booze
17.	carrot	donkey, rabbit, vegetable, orange, red
18.	plane	air, flat, fly, aero, crash
19.	television	radio, set, box, screen, aerial
20.	Chicago	America, riots, gangster, USA, gangsters

39. Seeing Colors

All human eyes work in the same way so that they can see the same colors. Yet different languages don't just have different words for colors, they recognize different basic colors. A basic color name consists of a single word like *red* rather than a phrase like *pillarbox red* and has a high frequency, *red* rather than *crimson* or *scarlet*.

The psychologists Brent Berlin and Paul Kay discovered that the different languages of the world used basic color names in terms of the scale shown on the next page. Some languages have the minimum of basic color names. Welsh, for instance, uses only the two color names at the left of the scale, *black* and *white*. Languages with one extra color name, such as Tiv (spoken in Nigeria), add *red* to the list. Languages with two more color names, such as Navaho, add *green* and *yellow*. And so on along the scale until they reach the maximum of eleven color names, found in Hebrew and English.

In other words, working backward from right to left on the scale, if a language has a word for *blue*, it also has one for *red*; if it has *brown*, it also has *blue*, and so on. But no language has *brown* without having *blue*; you can't leave anything out on the scale from left to right. The selection of basic color terms in a language is not random but follows the scale. Some languages have more color names, some less, but they are all related to this scale.

Of course it is perfectly possible to describe other colors in any language, say by using *light* and *dark*, *light red*, *dark green*, or by comparison with natural objects such as *sky blue*, *olive green*; languages always have a way of specifying such details when needed. It is only in the number of basic color names in everyday use that they differ.

As proof of how difficult it can be to visualize colors in another language, English people find it amazing that Japanese, as well as having two "blues" (*ao* and *mizuiro*), has two "greens" (*midori* and *kimidori*) all of which are quite distinct colors to a Japanese eye.

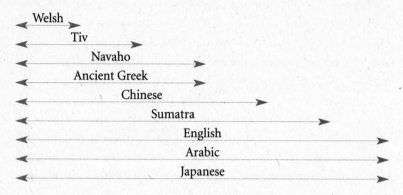

I	II	III	IV	V	VI
black		green			pink
white >	red >	yellow >	blue >	brown >	orange
					gray

So what happens when you learn another language? Do you still have the same feel for colors or do you start to "see" the colors named in the new language? One bilingual researcher, Panos Athanasopoulos, has shown that Greeks who know English categorize the "blues" differently from monolinguals. Another, Miho Sasaki, has shown the same for Japanese "greens." Learning another language changes the way you see the world, almost literally.

The order in which English children start to use color terms is also interesting:

red > green > black > white > orange > yellow > blue > pink > brown > purple

This looks rather like the Berlin and Kay scale. The first four color terms, *red*, *green*, *black*, and *white*, are all in the first five of the scale; three of the last four to be learned, *blue*, *pink* and *brown*, are in the last four of the scale. The exceptions are *gray*, which the children did not produce, and *purple*, which is not on the universal list at all, and so probably not a basic color term. Teaching young children their colors is in fact introducing them to the way that English handles color terms; there may be little point in jumping ahead on the scale or introducing non-basic terms until they have gone through the whole sequence.

40. Progenies of Learning
MALAPROPISMS

Malapropisms in speech are so named after Mrs. Malaprop, a character in Richard Sheridan's play *The Rivals* (1775), who made remarks like:

"I would by no means wish a daughter of mine to be a progeny of learning … I would send her, at nine years old, to a boarding-school, in order to learn a little ingenuity and artifice. Then, sir she should have a supercilious knowledge in accounts … but above all … she should be mistress of orthodoxy, that she might not mis-spell …"

In other words, Mrs. Malaprop tried to impress by using long words but chose wrong ones that had a vague resemblance.

A variation is Nell Sims, a housekeeper in a Perry Mason novel by Erle Stanley Gardner, *The Case of the Drowsy Mosquito* (1943), who garbled proverbs:

It's a case of one man's poison being another's meat.
Food preservation is the first law of nature.
A stitch in time is worth a pound of cure.
An eavesdropper gathers no moss.
Just a case of absence making the heart grow fonder of the bird in hand.

The serious point to this is how the mind organizes vocabulary into words with similar sounds and words with similar meanings. Psycholinguists such as Ann Cutler collect real-life slips of the tongue, such as:

We have a lovely Victorian condom set. (condiment)
Although murder is a form of suicide.
As long as I'm in my own little nit. (niche)

Hardly a minute passes without someone making a slip by using the wrong word – after all, there are thousands to choose from in a fraction of a second when you are speaking.

Psychiatrists like Freud see such slips as giving away secret thought processes:

A patient said she only saw her uncle in flagrante, meaning en passant.
A woman said her new English teacher showed that he would like to give her private lessons "*durch die Bluse*" [through the blouse] rather than "*durch die Blume*" [through flowers, i.e. indirectly].

Indeed, the media had a field day with former British prime minister Gordon Brown's slip in saying he was saving *the world* rather than *the British economy*.

41. Hanky-panky with Igglepiggle
REDUPLICATIVE WORDS

Some words in English simply repeat themselves, the second part being identical with the first, *pooh-pooh*; or repeating the first part with a change of vowel (*riff-raff*) or of consonant (*teeny-weeny*). These are called reduplicative words. Here are some everyday English examples:

Ordinary examples
Repeating without change

bye-bye	hush-hush
haha	blah blah
gaga	

Repeating with change of vowel

flip-flop	mish-mash
knick-knack	pitter-patter
sing-song	see-saw
ping-pong	criss-cross

Repeating with change of consonant

hurdy-gurdy	mumbo-jumbo
walky-talky	hanky-panky
hodgepodge	higgledy-piggledy
hocus-pocus	

A particularly rich source of such words is baby talk, the name for the kind of language parents speak to children everywhere in the world (see page 191). One reason is that children's early babbling often repeats the same syllable over and over – *gagagaga* – so parents may think they are making it easier for the child if they imitate his or her sounds: *See the pretty bow-wow!*

Baby talk

tum-tum	bow-wow
night-night	boo-hoowee-wee
neigh-neigh	moo-moo
baa-baa	choo-choo

Many attractive reduplicative words have died out or survive only in dialects. Here is a selection, in case you want to bring any back to life.

Obscure words

geepie-gawpie	a shadow picture (Orkney)
kitch-witch	a woman dressed in a frightening way (East Anglia; still the name of a shop in Colchester)
mal-scral	a caterpillar (Devon)
holums-jolums	all at once (Warwick)
whisky-frisky	drunk on whisky (American)
borus-snorus	happy go lucky (Dorset)
joukerie-cookerie	trickery (Scottish)
hangy-bangy	a good-for-nothing (Northumberland)
hitherum-ditherum	a drying wind (Scottish)
rumpum-scrumpum	an instrument like a banjo (Wiltshire)

42. Is the Sea Blue or Do I Just See It as Blue?

LINGUISTIC RELATIVITY

I look at the sea and I say it's blue; another person looks at it and says it's green. A Greek looks at a dark blue object and says it's *ble* and looks at a light blue object and says it's *ghalazio*. To an English speaker these are just variations of a single color – a dark Oxford blue, say, compared to a light sky blue. To the Greeks (and indeed to Italians, Russians, and many others) these are distinct colors, having both light and dark shades of their own, rather than variations of the same color.

So do speakers of Greek see differently from speakers of English, or do they just talk about what they see differently? Do human beings think differently or do they talk differently?

The question does not go away if we try to find objective reasons for these differences. The famous example is Inuit (Eskimo) words for snow, though there has long been controversy over the actual facts. English has one word, *snow*. The Inuit language Yupik has many words for different types of snow: fine snow is *kanevvluk*, snow on the ground is *qanikcaq*, fallen snow floating on water is *qanisqineq*, and so on. English people appear to think quite differently from Inuits about snow and indeed from those in other snow bound countries such as Greenland, as we see in Peter Høeg's novel *Miss Smilla's Feeling for Snow*.

But doesn't English also have *slush*, *sleet* and even *hail*, all more or less types of frozen water coming from the sky? Couldn't any skier quickly add to the list with *powder snow*, *spring snow*, *blue snow* (a sign of avalanches) and so on? These may consist of two-word phrases rather than one, but Inuit words are constructed on different principles from English words, by combining bits together into one long word.

Another example is *saltiness*. English has one word *salty*, but Bahasa Malaysia has a range, including *masin kitchup* (salty like soy sauce) and *masin maung* (horribly salty). In an experiment, Malaysians were able to detect the amount of salt in water much better than were speakers of English. Their language affects their sense of taste.

One aspect of life that we express when we speak is how what we say relates to where we are standing or sitting, our point of view in a literal sense. Suppose I am in London, standing on Trafalgar Square. I am facing the National Gallery. On my left is Canada House, on my right is South Africa House, and behind me is Whitehall, more or less.

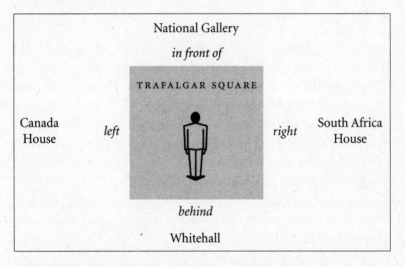

Now suppose I turn around, so that Whitehall is in front of me, the National Gallery is behind me, Canada House is on my right, and South Africa House is on my left. All the directions have switched with me as I turn because my point of view has changed; *left* and *right*, *in front* and *behind* have reversed. English, then, describes the situation in the basic terms *left*, *right*, *in front of*, *behind* as seen on the next page.

It seems perfectly obvious that the direction we are facing determines how we describe the scene around us. How could a

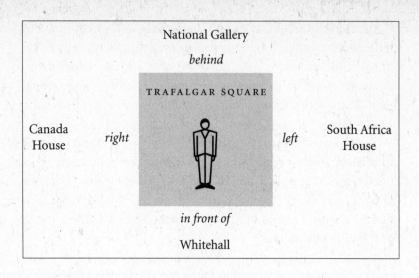

National Gallery

behind

TRAFALGAR SQUARE

Canada House   *right*   *left*   South Africa House

in front of

Whitehall

human being *not* see the world in terms of which way he or she was facing? Our bodies have a front and a back and a left and a right; our eyes are on the front; clearly we will see the world literally from our own perspective.

The technical name for this is "relative direction": the way the speaker is facing is the starting point; the direction-words used relate to this viewpoint. Up until the 1990s, linguists believed that everybody treated themselves as the center of the universe, linguistically speaking. Our position in time and space dictates what we mean when we express "left/right," "I/you," "now/then," "here/there" in any language.

But then the sociolinguist Steven Levinson discovered that Australian aboriginals do not locate themselves in space in this way. Take an aboriginal standing facing the National Gallery.

The aboriginal describes the situation in terms of the points of the compass. Canada House is in the west, South Africa House is in the east, the National Gallery is in the north, and Whitehall is in the south. The perspective comes not from his or her own viewpoint, but from the points of the compass.

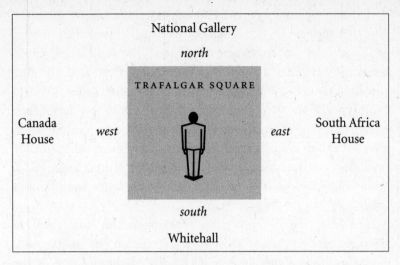

So, if the aboriginal turns round, nothing changes in the direction terms he or she uses.

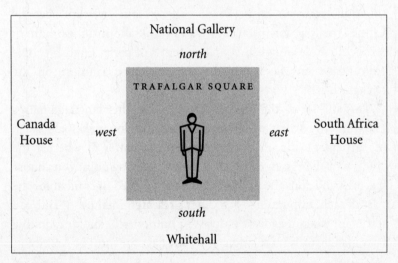

Despite now facing Whitehall, the aboriginal still describes the situation in exactly the same terms, *north*, *south*, *east*, and *west*. Directions for aboriginals are concerned with the geography of the world, with "absolute direction" unrelated to the way they are facing.

So human beings have two alternative ways of talking about the situation they are in, one based on relative direction, the other on absolute direction. An experiment tested how well people could find their way out of a jungle. Not surprisingly those with absolute direction fared better than those with relative direction. Of course both types of speaker can describe things in both fashions if they have to, but English speakers prefer relative direction except when they have to deal with maps, and it also depends on whether they are indoors or outdoors: *His desk is to the north of mine* sounds odd, while *That chestnut is to the north side of my garden* sounds more likely.

The idea that differences in speaking reflect differences in thinking has become known as linguistic relativity, by analogy with Einstein's ideas about time being relative to the position of the observer. Language and thinking are bound together and vary in all sorts of ways among the people of the world. One big divide in thinking seems to be between "eastern" and "western" people. Chinese people, for instance, tend to think about things more in terms of wholes, English people in terms of parts. English people concentrate on the foreground of a picture, Chinese on the background.

This still leaves the question open of whether language makes you think in particular ways or whether thinking makes you speak in particular ways. By and large this is a matter of whether the chicken or the egg came first. Whichever starting point you choose has pros and cons. Researchers have been locked in combat for the past decade, impugning each other's research methods ("Did you test them when they were indoors or outdoors?") and questioning how many words Inuit languages really have for snow or Arabic has for camels.

43. At a Loss for Words

APHASIA

The loss of the ability to use words is called aphasia. Since the mid-nineteenth century, aphasia has been found to be related to damage in the brain caused by injury, strokes etc., chiefly in two areas on the left side of the brain, named after their discoverers, Paul Broca and Carl Wernicke.

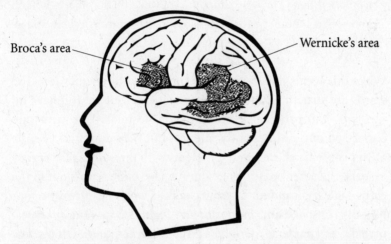

Broca's area — Wernicke's area

Damage to each of these areas results in different types of word loss. Here is a patient speaking who has damage to Broca's area, reported by Howard Gardner:

DOCTOR: Could you tell me, Mr. Ford, what you've been doing in the hospital?
PATIENT: Yes. Sure. Me go, er, uh, PT, nine o'cot, speech . . . two times . . . read . . . wr . . . ripe, er, rike, er, write . . . practice . . . getting better.

The content words (nouns, adjectives and the like) such as *speech* and *practice* are still there, but the structure words like *of* and *to* and the different forms of the pronouns *I/me/my* have gone. The words do not link together into anything larger than a two-word phrase such as *getting better*. Nevertheless it is still possible to understand something of what Mr. Ford is trying to say about his day in the hospital.

Here, on the other hand, is a patient with damage to Wernicke's area answering a similar question:

DOCTOR: What brings you to the hospital?

PATIENT: Boy, I'm sweating. I'm awful nervous, you know, once in a while I get caught up, I can't mention the tarripoi, a month ago, quite a little, I've done a lot well, I impose a lot, while, on the other hand, you know what I mean, I have to run around, look it over, trebbin and all that sort of stuff.

While this seems fluent, it doesn't connect with the question. The words are structured into a proper sequence but we still have no idea why the patient has come to the hospital. The words are connected into phrases and sentences but they don't make sense. Such people also have severe problems with the names of everyday objects. On other occasions he can manage other words not in the extract like *book* and *ear* but says *chair* for *table* and *knee* for *elbow*: he calls *clip plick* and *butter tubber*; for *ankle* he said *ankey, no mankle, no kankle*; for *fork* he said *tonsil, teller, tongue, fung*. The right connections between a word and its meaning have gone.

Until recently it was believed that damage to the right side of the brain did not affect language to the same extent as damage to the left side; both Broca's and Wernicke's areas are on the left. As broadly speaking the right brain handles emotions, damage to the right side can affect your ability to handle emotional aspects of language, such as the interpretation of emotion conveyed by intonation – the rise and fall of the voice in speech which often in English conveys emotional overtones: *nice* versus *nice* versus *nice*. The divorce rate is allegedly higher in right-side-damaged patients, as they don't convey or understand the same emotions as before and their spouses see this as rejection rather than as the after-effects of their injury.

44. How Old are Your Words?

THE VOCABULARY OF DIFFERENT GENERATIONS

Tick which word out of each pair you use most often. This should give an indication of how old you seem from your vocabulary. Answers are on page 284.

1. great	☐	all right	☐
2. bike	☐	cycle	☐
3. crappy	☐	terrible	☐
4. LP	☐	vinyl	☐
5. lousy	☐	bad	☐
6. fellow	☐	guy	☐
7. hammered	☐	sloshed	☐
8. TV	☐	television	☐
9. smashed	☐	wrecked	☐
10. cool	☐	excellent	☐
11. drunk	☐	tipsy	☐
12. stereo	☐	record player	☐

Some words do not die out, only the people who use them. We are labelled with the words of our generation and carry them on with us. But this explanation does not always work. A word like *chap*, to me very much an older-generation word, has been going strong since 1716. The sociolinguist William Labov talks of "age-grading": speakers adopt the words they think suitable to their years, just as in television advertisements retired men put on cardigans to potter in the garden. So *chap* may be permanently associated with the old and we start to use it when, say, we apply for our free bus pass. Young people too may use words because they believe they are a badge of youth: for example, *pissed* and *telly*.

When I gave a questionnaire to people of different ages, the words they associated with older people were *record player*, *tipsy* and *granny*, with younger people *telly*, *pissed*, and *nan*. The words that they produced for drunk were interesting in that the distinctive word for older people was *sozzled*, while younger people supplied a large range of terms: *pissed, slaughtered, paralytic, legless, wrecked, plastered, hammered, nutted, out of 'er 'ead, drunk as a skunk*, and *out of it*.

45. The Birdiest Bird

PROTOTYPES

If you had to explain to someone what a bird was, which of these drawings would you point to?

Prototype theory, proposed by the psychologist Eleanor Rosch, looks at the way in which we choose representatives of particular categories – how you chose the birdiest bird out of the images above. Rosch claimed that rather than all the examples of a category being equal, each category has a central example that stands out as most typical, which she called the prototype. All birds are not the same; some are more or less "birdy." A robin is the birdiest of them all; a goldfinch isn't quite so birdy, and an emu only just squeezes in as a bird as it doesn't even fly. Each of the categories in our minds has a prototype, whether birds, furniture, or anything else. The birds or the furniture that we see fit the prototypes better or worse. Later research by the psychologist Lawrence Barsalou claims that we visualize the prototype in a particular situation or movement. When you think of a bird, is it flying or is it perched? The meaning for us includes how we visualize the object.

Prototype theory is one way of thinking about how our minds organize vocabulary, not just for English but for all languages. The prototypes in our mind govern how we understand the world around us.

46. Tasting the Worm
SPOONERISMS

The Rev. Dr. Spooner, Warden of New College, Oxford, from 1903 to 1930, once proposed a toast to *Our queer dean*, announced a hymn as *Kinkering Kongs their titles take*, and told a student, *You have deliberately tasted two worms. You have hissed my mystery lectures and you will have to leave on the next town drain*. Hence swapping the initial sounds of two words became known as a spoonerism. Most of these examples are now thought to be apocryphal, though Spooner clearly did use spoonerisms in real life.

Spoonerisms are in fact common in everyday speech and were well known long before Spooner; only when the exchange of sounds makes some sort of sense do we notice it. Putting together a sentence involves grammar, words, and sounds. If these elements get out of step and the sentence has two words with swappable initial sounds, you get a spoonerism.

Sometimes it is the two consonants that get swapped: *waste terms > taste worms*; sometimes the first vowel after the consonant: *Conquering Kings > Kinkering Kongs*. This is different from malapropisms, in which whole words are exchanged (see page 104) and different also from the process in which two sounds are exchanged within the word (metathesis), such as *grass* from *gars*, exchanging "a" and "r" – a common enough mistake in typing or writing, like *hte* for *the* or *form* for *from*.

A person who is constantly producing spoonerisms, such as Warden Spooner, may have a speech defect. But they are also produced on purpose. A vast selection of contrived spoonerisms can be found, such as:

It is kisstomary to cuss the bride.

Chork pocks

Par cark (cited as a sign of dyslexia by the Dyslexia Institute)

Hoobert Heever

I'd rather have a bottle in front of me than a frontal lobotomy
(attributed to both Dorothy Parker and to W. C. Fields)

Beeping Sleauty

Daughtiful beauter

Roaring with pain

A well-boiled icicle

47. Tip of the Tongue Test

In the Tip of the Tongue Test you have to guess the right word. The length of the space does not correspond to the number of missing letters. First cover everything but the definition of the first word and the space after it with a sheet of paper. If you know the word, write it down; if you are half sure, write down a guess. If you don't know the word, move the paper down a line to see one letter; write it down if you know it or write down a guess. And so on until you either guess the word or see the right answer. Then move down to see the right answer.

1. an instrument used for measuring the angle of the sun, moon and stars at sea

   ....

   s..

   s...t

   s.............t.................t

   sextant

2. semicircular or many-sided recess, with an arched or domed roof

   ....

   ......p............

   ......p..........e

   ap...........e

   apse

3. an underground conduit for drainage, a common sewer

....

.........................a

...........a...........a

c...........a...........a

cloaca

4. a fragrant drug that melts almost like wax, commonly used
both as a perfume and a cordial

....

a...........................

a...........................s

a...........g...........s

ambergris

5. a small boat with oars that is found in China

....

...........................n

...........p...........n

s...........p...........n

sampan

6. sad and solemn by nature

....

s...........................

s...........................e

s...........r...........e

saturnine

7. the meaning is unmistakable

....

......................................l

u....................................l

u................q................l

unequivocal

8. making a picture by cutting into a surface

....

i......................................

i................g................

i................g................o

intaglio

9. a young female water spirit

....

n......................................

n................a................

n................a....d

naiad

10. to continually change your opinion

....

................................e

................i................e

v................i................e

vacillate

The test is trying to induce a "tip of the tongue" (TOT) state. It is concerned with what happens when you *almost* know a word – when it's on the tip of your tongue. The words are taken from the original experiment by the psycholinguists Roger Brown and David McNeil.

If you reacted like most people in a TOT state, you knew what the first letter of the word was, possibly the last letter, but you didn't know anything in the middle. Our minds store the word with a particular emphasis on the beginning and the end. It's like peering through a dirty window that makes everything in the middle a blur. We remember a word as a pattern with the first part most visible – we know what it starts with but we don't know how it goes on. One explanation for this is that other related words block access to the exact word in the memory; brain studies have found that people activate their visual memory in trying to remember the appearance of the word.

48. "Can the Can" (Suzi Quatro)

WORDS AND MULTIPLE MEANINGS

Languages can use a limited number of sounds to make words, restricted by what human beings can produce and hear. So, all too often, words that look or sound exactly the same have totally different meanings. Languages like Chinese have an advantage in that written characters have little connection with the spoken form; similar-sounding words will look very different in writing. In English, though, the same sequence of sounds can make up several different words.

Take the word *can*. As a noun, *can* may mean:

- "a container for liquids," *a milk-can*
- "a cylindrical metal container," *trashcan*
- "the buttocks," *sitting on my can*
- "a measure of capacity," *a can of oil*
- "a prison," *he's in the can*
- "a metal container for preserving food," *a can of beans*

The connections between these diverse senses of *can* are tenuous.

But what about *can* as a verb? Some of its meanings are naturally related to the noun:

- "to put in a can," *he canned the beans*
- "to preserve on film," *she canned the shot*

Others seem unrelated:

- "to expel," *he was canned*
- "to stop," *can that noise!*

The most common use of *can* is undoubtedly as an auxiliary verb:

- "to know how to do something," *I can swim*
- "possibility," *can you open the door for me?*

The auxiliary *can* is a structure word whose role is grammatical. Like other auxiliaries, it moves in the sentence to form questions: *He can swim > Can he swim?*, unlike ordinary verbs, *He swims > Swims he?*

So what counts as a word here? At the very least *can* seems like three words: noun, verb and auxiliary. But adding up the meanings gets twelve using only those listed here.

It is not that dictionaries have dreamed up this information. Anybody who speaks English knows all of these meanings of *can*, without going on to technical meanings such as *can* for the sheathing of nuclear fuel or phrases such as *carry the can*. The dictionary in our heads is nearly as complicated as the paper dictionary; the same three letters can lead everywhere from getting fired to prison to baked beans.

49. Can Sounds and Letters Have Meanings in Themselves?

SOUND SYMBOLISM IN WORDS

Usually we think of meaning as belonging to whole words like *beer* rather than to bits of words like *ee* or *er*. We can accept that word endings like *-ing* or *-ly* have some sort of meaning; *row* means something different from *rowing*, *sad* from *sadly*. But we don't usually find meaning in single letters or sounds, apart perhaps from *I* and *a*, which are words in their own right.

Yet some combinations of sounds or letters do seem to go with particular meanings in a handful of English words:

"sn-" – means something to do with breathing and the nose or mouth: *snore, sneer, sniff, snot, sneeze, snort, snuffle, sniffles, snob, snuff, snout, snarl, snicker, snigger, snivel, snorkel, snooze, snooty, snigger, snub.* (28 percent of words starting with *sn-* have this overtone)

"tw-" – something to do with pinching or twisting: *tweak, twirl, twist, tweezers, twiddle, twine*

"-ip" – light blows: *nip, clip*

"-ous" – lip smacking: *luscious, delicious, scrumptious, voluptuous*

"-tion" – no clear meaning (apart from going with abstract nouns) but vital in reggae lyrics and political discourse: *revolution, generation, appreciation, consideration, nation, satisfaction, jubilation, globalization, marketization, theorization, problematization*

"sq-" – something unpleasant to do with liquid and impact: *squash, squish, squeeze, squelch, squirt, squirm, squat*

"gl-" – something to do with seeing things and reflected light: *glare, glitter, gleam, glimmer, glint, glow, glare, glitz, glass, glance, glimpse, glaze, gloom, glisten, gloss* (39 percent of words with *gl-* have to do with light in some way)

These associations between sounds and meanings can't be a total coincidence, particularly the words starting with *gl-* and *sn-*. We may work out these correspondences between sounds and meanings subconsciously from hearing the existing words and then applying the rule to new ones. Hearing words like *glare* and *glint* makes us anticipate that any word starting with *gl-* will have something to do with light.

50. Concordancing
FINDING OUT ABOUT WORDS

Concordancing is a way of using the computer to find out how words behave. It is used by dictionary makers, language teachers and others to find out how often words occur and what other words they go with, and to work out their meanings from the sentences in which they occur. Researchers in children's language see what words children are using; researchers in second-language acquisition find out learners' mistakes; non-native students of English find out aspects of words practically rather than by looking them up in a dictionary. It is used informally on many pages of this book.

To concordance vocabulary, you first need a set of texts in electronic form: this is your "corpus." A corpus of written language is now easy to collect over the Internet from sites like Project Gutenberg with complete novels, from newspaper archives, and the like. Anybody can make their own database of written language; any digital text you can lay your hand on will do, whether a novel by P. G. Wodehouse or the speeches of Daniel Webster. It is more difficult to get a corpus of spoken language, as this means first recording it, then laboriously writing it down – according to one rule of thumb, an hour of tape takes eighteen hours to transcribe.

Then you need a computer program to carry out the analysis. Google can be used for a simple count of words. Feed in *immunosurveillance* and it lists 58,900 pages, then feed in *phone* and it lists 933 million; so we know something of their relative frequency. But of course Google is counting pages, not words themselves, and a word may be used many times on a single page. Google also has many pages in languages other than English, as I found to my cost when I tried to google *til* as a spelling mistake for *till* and discovered that it is a common Scandinavian word.

A program that is specially designed to do this is called a concordancer. Essentially this counts words and works out which words occur together. Some concordancers are free on the Internet – search for *Compleat Lexical Tutor* if you're interested; others, like *WordSmith*, used in this book, cost reasonable sums; the state of the art for professional dictionary makers is *Sketch Engine*, also available for a comparatively small amount. After you've mastered how the program works, you can start asking it questions about your corpus.

P. G. Wodehouse's 1919 book *My Man Jeeves*, downloadable from the Gutenberg Project, can be a test case of a corpus. The novel is 51,431 running words long and has 5,017 different words – information instantly provided by the concordancer.

The easiest question to settle is what are the most frequent words in the novel. The top twenty words are:

the, I, to, a, and, of, you, it, was, he, in, that, said, had, me, on, for, at, his, with

In other words, the top twenty are ordinary structure words of English, which are very frequent in any piece of written English.

But it is also possible to focus on a particular word. Let us take *girl*, prominent in any P. G. Wodehouse novel. Sure enough, *girl* occurs fifty times, *girls* five times and *girl's* six times, sixty-one times in total. So *girl* effectively occurs once every 869 words. In the British National Corpus (BNC), which contains 100 million running words, the rate for *girl* is, however, one in 3,942 words. P. G. Wodehouse is thus using the word *girl* 4.5 times more than it is generally used in English. Of course, the word might be common to this style of writing or to this period of English rather than an idiosyncrasy of this author's style.

How does P. G. Wodehouse actually use the word *girl*? The most useful information that a concordancer provides is a list of all the examples of *girl* in the corpus along with their surrounding context. Here are the first five occurrences of *girl* in the novel. The test word *girl* appears centered in the middle of the line. It does take a while to make sense of such displays.

1.	stop young Gussie marrying a	**girl**	on the vaudeville stage, and
2.	one afternoon, shooing a	**girl**	in front of him, and
3.	scared, Mr. Wooster," said the	**girl.**	"We were hoping that you
4.	"Thank you, sir." The	**girl**	made an objection. "But
5.	of Gussie and the vaudeville	**girl**	was still fresh in my

This is called a KWIC display – Key Word In Context. At first it looks strange, giving about six words before and after the key word *girl*, cut off in mid-word and mid-sentence. But these chunks often have all the information you need to study the word. If you need more, you can expand any example. For instance, No. 5 becomes in full:

And the recollection of my Aunt Agatha's attitude in the ma*tter of Gussie and the vaudeville girl was still fresh in my mind.*

Examples 1 and 2 show that *girl* goes with the article *a*, which may be all you need if you are looking for proof that it is a certain kind of noun, namely "countable." It also shows that *girl* can be the object of the verb *marry* within a phrase *young Gussie marrying a girl*, a high-frequency collocation.

The information from this example of the word *girl* seems banal. But when it is multiplied by the sixty-one examples in the novel, it tells you more; the 25,366 examples of *girl* and *girls* in the BNC tell you still more.

What words come near to *girl* in the text? Taking ten words before and after every occurrence of *girl* and leaving out function words like *the*, the words that often occur in the vicinity of *girl* are *stage, quarrel, man, vaudeville, love, married, engaged*, and *pretty* – a fairly good impression of young women's activities in P. G. Wodehouse books. For a dictionary maker, this gives a good idea what *girl* meant in this kind of book at a particular period of time.

As a comparison from the same decade, let us take Virginia Woolf's 1915 novel *The Voyage Out*, 137,530 words long with 9,542 different words. Already the fact that it has twice as many individual words as *My Man Jeeves* suggests it is more demanding of the reader. Forms of *girl* occur forty-eight times, or once every 2,865 words, far less than in P. G. Wodehouse. Here are the first five examples of *girl* in Woolf.

1.	her boy was like her and her	**girl**	like Ridley. As for brains,
2.	Rachel was an unlicked	**girl,**	no doubt prolific of confide
3.	and come cringing to a	**girl**	because she wanted to sit
4.	a child for her health; as a	**girl**	and a young woman was
5.	and, as it happened, the only	**girl**	she knew well was a religious

Nothing about *vaudeville* here! The contexts for *girl* give a quite different impression from Wodehouse.

To make this more solid, we can compare the proportion of times the two authors use a word. P. G. Wodehouse uses *absolutely* and *pretty* ten times as often as Virginia Woolf does, *boy* eight times as often, *girl* five times as often, and *old* 3.5 times as often. In reverse, Virginia Woolf uses *people* and *Mrs.* nine times more often, *men* and *women* five times more often, and *world* four times more often. So, while P. G. Wodehouse writes about boys and girls, Virginia Woolf writes about men and women.

Some of the differences the computer throws up may be trivial. Others raise questions one wouldn't otherwise have thought of. Why, for instance, does P. G. Wodehouse use the pronoun *I* three times as often as Virginia Woolf does? Is it just that his characters spend their time in light badinage about each other, or is it a more profound aspect of their worldviews?

And this is only the tip of the iceberg. Vast amounts of statistical comparisons can be produced at the touch of a mouse. Concordancers provide an instant way of comparing frequencies between any pair of texts that you can enter in digital form. They are crucial also in studying the grammatical patterns of the language, outside the scope of this book. *Sketch Engine*, for instance, goes far beyond simple counting: a word sketch it produced for the word *impression* tells you it is usually an object of the verb *to make an impression*, that it goes with adjectives such as *lasting* and *misleading*, and that it occurs in phrases such as *an impression of objectivity/strength/progress*. Nor is it just dictionary makers who find it useful. Other beneficiaries include researchers looking for mistakes made by users of English, literary critics establishing who wrote a text, and forensic linguists trying to test someone's guilt in a court of law.

51. Apes and Words

Can apes use words? Perhaps the reason why they don't say anything is because no one has encouraged them to or because they can't make the right sounds. One way around this is to teach them Yerkish, an artificial language that displays word signs on a computer screen when an ape hits a keyboard. Hit a ☾ and you get dessert; hit a ⟨∧⟩ and you get a coconut. An ape called Sherman would hit the three symbols "Want orange drink." After getting the drink, he typed "Pour orange drink" and then requested "Give straw." He had been taught how to communicate through word signs without involving actual speech.

A pigmy chimpanzee called Kanzi watched his mother being taught Yerkish but seemed to take little interest in what was going on. However, when the mother went away temporarily, Kanzi showed that he had picked up Yerkish simply by observing his mother being taught. By the age of five years he could handle about 150 "words." At six he could respond successfully to around 300 different "sentences." One successful routine involved him naming one of seventeen possible locations in the surrounding estate, say "tree-house," and then leading a human escort to the spot. Clearly Kanzi could communicate to an extent, even if he was mostly interested in food.

An alternative way of training apes teaches them the words of human sign language, thus bypassing their physical inability to produce human speech sounds. By the age of five and a half, a gorilla called Koko had mastered 246 signs of American Sign Language (ASL), such as word signs for "alligator," "cake," "small," and "pour," and had started to make up "sentences" such as "Food-more," "Me-up-hurry," and "No-gorilla."

But are these apes really using anything like a human language? Their "sentences" do not have the almost error-free word order that a human child rapidly develops. Good as Koko was at getting the adjective in front of the noun, as in "dirty taste," he nevertheless was wrong about 25 percent of the time, i.e. "taste dirty," a far greater error rate than any human child.

Telling evidence against apes using language came from these same experiments. Human sign languages like American Sign Language have rules about where the gesture starts and where it finishes; the signs are not just natural gestures but highly stylized. But the signing apes treat a sign as a whole, not as a conventional sign; they use natural gestures rather than the abstract signs of sign language.

So can apes really use words? In a sense they link strings of words to particular things and actions. But no ape has ever acquired the ability to make new remarks about anything that he or she want to say. Tomorrow's football match, the discovery of a new particle in physics, the reality of alien abductions can all be discussed in any human language even if they have never been talked about before and do not actually exist. Human beings take this creativity for granted as their natural birthright, but it is unknown to other animals. Apes can indeed be taught to use a limited range of word signs for communication in a small number of situations, but no one has yet taught them the limitless potential of human language.

One day of Sherman's Yerkish computer sentences translated into English, in order of frequency

Out room Pour orange drink Austin [another chimp] Open Sue [a researcher] M&M [candy] Give Columbus Stick Columbus Room out Outdoors Gone Wrench Room Give out room Money Milk Magnet Give Sherman M&M Sherman out room Want orange drink Give open Tickle Door Sherman give M&M Sherman M&M Sherman room out Give pudding Scare Sweet potato Give pour drink Slide Door Austin Yes Sue Go outdoors Orange drink Sponge Juice Blanket Key No Give money Give milk Yes

52. Word Games with Restricted Production

Restricted-production games require the player to control their spontaneous speech in one way or another. A modern example, *Just a Minute*, a British radio version of a traditional game, requires celebrities to speak for a minute without "hesitation, repetition, or deviation." Though it is commendable to encourage speakers not to deviate, hesitation can be meaningful for dramatic effect, which should not be eliminated or may be a form of stuttering. Repetition of the same word can be effective – listen to any politician's three-fold repetition of *education, education, education*. The radio programme is designed to show off the wit and skill of the personalities involved, rather than for any point to the game itself.

Another type of restricted-production game was seen in the "Yes/No Interlude" on TV in the *Take Your Pick* television quiz show, in which contestants were banned from answering *yes* or *no* to questions put to them for one minute. More intellectual versions might involve banning all words that start with "e," have Latin roots, or are used in cookery. A tour de force of restricted-production was the 300-page novel *La Disparition* (translated by Gilbert Adair as *A Void*) written by Georges Pérec in French entirely without the letter "e."

53. Chaucer's Words

According to the *Oxford English Dictionary*, 2,004 words of English were first used by Geoffrey Chaucer in the late fourteenth century. As he wrote so much, *The Canterbury Tales* alone containing around 260,000 words, it may be that he was just the first person to use a word in public writing and was using words common in everyday speech. He can hardly have invented words such as *dung-cart*, *box*, or *trench*, even if he is the first person recorded to have used them.

Here is a selection of some of Chaucer's new words that are still

absence	dung-cart	jolliness	rumor
accident	effect (noun)	latitude	scissors
add	elixir	laxative	session
agree	examination	Martian	snort (verb)
bagpipe	femininity	milksop	superstitious
bed-head	finally	miscarry	theater
blunder (verb)	flute	nod (verb)	trench
border	funeral	notify	universe
box	galaxy	obscure	utility
chant (verb)	gaze (verb)	observe	vacation
cholera	glow (verb)	outrageous	veal
chuck (verb)	hernia	peregrine	village
cinnamon	horizon	perpendicular	vitriol
desk	increase (noun)	Persian	vulgar
digestion	infect (verb)	princess	wallet
dishonest	ingot	resolve (verb)	wildness

in use today:

Many words that appeared first in Chaucer's works did not catch on and have dropped out of our vocabulary, such as:

besmottered	corrumpable	displeasant
gastness	horsely	jangleress
necessarious	rete	withinforth

Some Chaucerian novelties reflect the twin influences in fourteenth-century England of French as the language of the ruling class and Latin as the language of education and scholarship – *examination*, *absence*, and *perpendicular*, often distinctly longer than the earlier Old English words.

Yet English was also open to other languages. For example, some of Chaucer's words come from Arabic through trade and Arabic science:

| almanac | alkali | amalgam | Arabic | borax |
| checkmate | damask | nadir | satin | tartar |

54. Igpay Atinlay

PIG LATIN

One way of playing with language is to code it into a slightly different form, sometimes for the fun of it, sometimes to conceal what is being said from people who do not know the rules. Parents, for example, spell out words so that their children do not follow what is being said: *It's A.U.N.T. K.A.T.E. on the phone.*

A classic form this takes is Pig Latin, which has a history going back several centuries. The rules of Pig Latin are straightforward, even if it takes practice to use them fluently:

- if a word starts with a vowel (*a, e, i, o, u*), add *-ay* to the end: *ask > askay; elephant > elephantay; ink > inkay; on > onnay; umpire > umpireay*
- if a word starts with a consonant (*bcdfg…*), move the first sound to the end of the word and then add *-ay*: *time > imetay; data > ataday; Gordon > ordongay; car > arcay*

Here are some titles of Abba songs to practise on:

aterlooway	upersay oopertray
oneymay oneymay oneymay	aketay aay ancechay onay emay
ankthay ouyay orfay ethay usicmay	ethay amenay ofay ethay amegay
ammamay iamay	ancingday eenquay
ernandofay	Iay avehay aay eamdray

There are two "dialects" of Pig Latin. Suppose you had to turn *cute* into Pig Latin, would you say *yutecay* or *utecay*? If you say *yutecay*, you are a Dialect A speaker: you treat the opening written consonant "c" of *cute* as having two spoken consonants "k" and "y," "kyoute"; moving the first consonant "k" produces *yutecay*. If you say *utecay*, you are a Dialect B person: you treat the opening "c" of

138

cute as "k," "kute," and get *utecay*, ignoring the "y" sound. The same applies to words starting with two consonants like *blue*, "bl" and *twist*, "tw": Dialect A speakers move only the first consonant, getting *luebay* and *wisttay*; Dialect B speakers move both sounds, getting *ueblay* and *isttway*.

At one level this is only a letter game, like *I-Spy*. However, it shows the different ways in which speakers handle English sounds. If you asked them to count the sounds in *cute*, Dialect A speakers would say it has four – "k," "y," "u" and "t," Dialect B speakers three – "ky," "u" and "t": they are hearing the language in different ways.

This is important because the combinations of consonants possible at the beginning of English words like "str-" as in *strike* differ from the usual consonant combinations. For example, "m" and "n" do not occur in combination with any other consonant than "s" – you can say *smile* and *sneeze* but you can't say *bneeze*, *tneeze* or *rneeze*. The fact that people mentally break "sn-" up into separate sounds shows that they are treating them separately rather than as a combined sound.

Reading relies partly on being able to work out the sequence of sounds in a word. Breaking up the sounds of a word and then moving the first one to the end involves isolating the initial sound from the rest; children are still only 75 percent accurate at this by the age of nine. So Pig Latin tests your ability to segment the sounds of words and has indeed been used as a way of assessing reading ability; poor readers are half as good at Pig Latin as average readers.

55. Forming New Words

Many new words are constructed out of the basic words in the language through a limited number of processes, called in general "derivation." There are five main processes, some of which are dealt with separately in this book.

1. **Suffixes** are added to the end of words with similar effects: *-ness* classes the word as a noun (*blackness*, *happiness*); *-al* as a noun (*arrival*) or an adjective (*partial.*) English suffixes are also used grammatically, such as *-s* in *books* for plural or *-ed* in *waited* for past tense. At other times they show the grammatical class of a word: *sad* is an adjective (*a sad fate*) but adding a *-ly* yields an adverb, *sadly*.

2. **Prefixes** are added at the beginning of the word to create a new word with an added meaning: *re-* is added to get *redo*, *replay*, *refurnish*, and *refinance*. We are no longer conscious of the prefix in earlier creations such as *relate*, *redemption*, *refrain*, etc. Other prefixes include *post- (postnatal, postpone)*; *in- (input, insure)*; *ex- (expatriate, ex-wife)*, and many others. Popular prefixes recently are *e-* as in *e-mail*, *mc as* in *mcjob* and *i-* as in *iPhone*.

3. **Compounds** are formed by combining two words to get a new word with a distinctive meaning: *tea + time* gives *teatime*, *back + rub* gives *backrub*, *base + ball* gives *baseball*, etc. The links between the two words vary considerably: a *goldfish* is colored gold but a *goldsmith* isn't; *uphold* is to "hold up" but *upbeat* is not to "beat up," as developed on pages 196–98.

4. **Conversion** is when a word is converted to a new grammatical class. For example, the preposition *up* is clearly a verb in *he upped the stakes*, the verb *read* is used as a noun in *a good read*, the adjective *green* as a noun in *the Greens*. Some of these conversions are so old that we are no longer aware of them; we

only notice modern inventions like teenagers' *big up*, meaning "to praise."

5. **Infixes** occur in the middles of words and are extremely rare in English (see pages 226). The rapper Snoop Dogg is famous for using *izz* and *izzle* as infixes: *hizzouse* (house), *ahizzlead* (ahead).

Derivation will obviously attract writers who like to play with words. Can you guess the creators of the following? Answers on page 285.

			Douglas Coupland	Terry Pratchett	P. G. Wodehouse	Anthony Burgess
suffixes	1.	Omnianism	☐	☐	☐	☐
	2.	gorgeosity	☐	☐	☐	☐
	3.	soup-platey	☐	☐	☐	☐
prefixes	4.	teleparablizing	☐	☐	☐	☐
	5.	ultra-violence	☐	☐	☐	☐
	6.	ambi-sinister	☐	☐	☐	☐
compounds	7.	kick-boots	☐	☐	☐	☐
	8.	downnesting	☐	☐	☐	☐
	9.	black-on-black eyes	☐	☐	☐	☐
conversion	10.	upping with the lark	☐	☐	☐	☐
infixes	11.	emallgration	☐	☐	☐	☐

56. Which Words Change Historically?

Various mathematical formulas have been applied to find out the types of word that change most as a language develops. The crucial factor seems to be that the more often a word is used, the less likely it is to be replaced by a new one. So *man* has a high frequency and has been with us in essentially the same form since before the Norman Conquest. *Wergild*, "a person's estimated value for compensation purposes," died out for lack of use (apart from the occasional vampire novel) and the idea has to be expressed in an awkward paraphrase.

Words that are used all the time have so much inertia that they can't be changed; words that are seldom used have little inertia. Numbers like *two* and pronouns like *I* are unlikely to change their pronunciation as they're said so often; rarer nouns like *Kenya* or *zebra* are more likely to change. The side effect is that common words are most likely to break the rules: *man* and *child* have kept their irregular plurals *men* and *children* since Old English. The most frequent verb in English is *to be*, with its different forms making up four of the top twenty words for English. And of course *to be* also has a highly irregular present tense, *am/is/are*; it is the only verb in English with different past-tense forms for singular *was* and plural *were*, and is the only verb that still sometimes has a subjunctive form, *If I were you*.

57. Proper English Food?

THE HISTORY OF FOOD WORDS

Probably much the same food was eaten by most people in England for a thousand years. Yet many current words for food came into English comparatively recently. The dates of their first occurrence provide a potted history of invasions, discoveries, colonization, trade, and the spread of package holidays.

Century	Words
	(OE = Old English; F = French; some have uncertain sources)
pre-1066	lamb, bean, apple, pear, pea, bread, ale, wine (all OE)
13th	beer (OE)
14th	beef (F), veal (F)
15th	steak (Norse?), peach (F), orange (F), lemon (F), sausage (F)
16th	curry (Tamil), potato (Spanish), banana (Spanish/F), coffee (Arabic), tea (Chinese via Dutch?), pizza (Italian), gooseberry (Dutch?)
17th	soup (F), coulis (F), tomato (F)
18th	stew (F), gin (Dutch), whisky (Gaelic), waffle (Dutch)
19th	spaghetti (Italian), padum (Tamil), hamburger (German), salami (Italian), panettone (Italian)
20th	sushi (Japanese), chow mein (Chinese), tapas (Spanish), bruschetta (Italian), balti (Hindi/Punjabi?)
21st	ciabatta (Italian)

It is surprising how long some of these terms have been around; *spaghetti*, *hamburger*, and *panettone* seem more twentieth than nineteenth century. Though *coulis* looks modern, it has been in use since the seventeenth century. Were people in the sixteenth century really eating *curries* and *pizzas*, the staple British diet of the 1990s?

In reverse, some names occur surprisingly late: *soup* came from French in 1653, though there must have been soup before then.

An odd consequence of the centuries-long coexistence of English and French in England is that there are often two words for the same thing, one from Old English to describe the living animal, the other from French to describe parts of it that are dead and can be cooked.

Alive (OE)	Dead and cookable (mostly F)
sheep	mutton (but lamb OE)
cow	beef, veal
deer	venison
pig	pork, ham, gammon, bacon

58. What Does Oprah Winfrey Mean to You?

THE SEMANTIC DIFFERENTIAL TEST

Words have many different types of meaning, one of which is measured by the Semantic Differential Test. This evaluates the overtones that go with a word, its connotations rather than its main meaning. Try the following example to see how it works.

What does Oprah Winfrey mean to you?
Fill in how much you think Oprah Winfrey is related to the concepts on each of the following scales.

		7	6	5	4	3	2	1	
1.	fair	O	O	O	O	O	O	O	unfair
2.	strong	O	O	O	O	O	O	O	weak
3.	fast	O	O	O	O	O	O	O	slow
4.	clean	O	O	O	O	O	O	O	dirty
5.	hard	O	O	O	O	O	O	O	soft
6.	bright	O	O	O	O	O	O	O	dark
7.	pleasant	O	O	O	O	O	O	O	unpleasant
8.	heavy	O	O	O	O	O	O	O	light
9.	active	O	O	O	O	O	O	O	passive
10.	sweet	O	O	O	O	O	O	O	sour
11.	large	O	O	O	O	O	O	O	small
12.	sharp	O	O	O	O	O	O	O	dull

Now:
- add up the scores for 1, 4, 7, 10: this is called the **evaluation factor** ....
- add up the scores for 2, 5, 8, 11: this is the **potency factor** ....
- add up the scores for 3, 6, 9, 12: this is the **activity factor** ....

So to you, Oprah Winfrey is:

............/28 evaluation

............/28 potency

............/28 activity

These are called the three dimensions of "semantic space." They form an imaginary three-dimensional cube in which the concept being tested gets a single position defined by the three coordinates.

Any concept can be measured in this way. The original research tested concepts ranging from *dawn* to *engine* to *capital punishment*, using seventy-six scales instead of the twelve used here.

Semantic differential tests have been around since the 1950s. Advertisers test what people think of their products. Psycho-analysts look at differences between the personalities of people with multiple-personality disorder. Eve, the famous patient with multiple personalities, had very different scores for the same word according to which of her three personalities was dominant at the time.

The difficulty with using the technique to study the meaning of words is that none of the scales say who or what Oprah Winfrey actually *is* – the host of a TV show. They reveal how you evaluate her but not the meaning in the usual sense in which Oprah Winfrey refers to a particular person hosting an internationally syndicated talk show. So Semantic Differential Tests are good at showing changes in what people think – vital to advertisers, politicians and the like, where opinions are all that count, but are more or less useless to dictionary makers who need to know what words mean and how they are used.

Now you can do the same test using a politician or any other concept available in English – a new type of word game to play at parties.

What does .... mean to you?

Fill in how much .... is related to the concepts on each of the following scales.

		7	6	5	4	3	2	1	
1.	fair	O	O	O	O	O	O	O	unfair
2.	strong	O	O	O	O	O	O	O	weak
3.	fast	O	O	O	O	O	O	O	slow
4.	clean	O	O	O	O	O	O	O	dirty
5.	hard	O	O	O	O	O	O	O	soft
6.	bright	O	O	O	O	O	O	O	dark
7.	pleasant	O	O	O	O	O	O	O	unpleasant
8.	heavy	O	O	O	O	O	O	O	light
9.	active	O	O	O	O	O	O	O	passive
10.	sweet	O	O	O	O	O	O	O	sour
11.	large	O	O	O	O	O	O	O	small
12.	sharp	O	O	O	O	O	O	O	dull

Dimensions

............/28 evaluation

............/28 potency

............/28 activity

59. Stressed-out Nouns

Usually an English content word such as a noun or a verb has the stress on the same syllable whenever it is said: *Ireland* is pronounced _Ireland_, not *Ireland*, except in unusual circumstances like checking the pronunciation, *Did you say Ireland?*

However, stress patterns vary in some words according to their role in the sentence: *perfect* is stressed on the first syllable when it's an adjective: *a _perfect_ meal*, on the second when it's a verb: *she perfected her serve*. Typically this stress shift occurs when the first syllable is a prefix, such as *re-*, *con-*, *in-*, etc.

Stressed first syllable noun/adjective		Stressed second syllable verb	
contrast	What a contrast!	_contrast_	They contrast life with death.
absent	He's absent today.	_absent_	He absented himself.
combine	In July he rented a combine.	_combine_	She combined wit with humor.
insult	What an insult!	_insult_	He insulted me.
present	She gave him a present.	_present_	He presented the prize.
convict	The convict escaped.	_convict_	The judge convicted him.
rebel	Rebel without a cause	_rebel_	He rebelled against the state.
record	They released a record.	_record_	This call is being recorded.

Stressed first syllable noun/adjective		Stressed second syllable verb	
_pro_ceeds	the proceeds from the robbery	pro_ceeds_	The car proceeded down the Mall.
_pro_phecy	The prophecy of the end of the world	pro_phesy_	They prophesy the end of the world in July.
_sur_vey	They requested a survey.	sur_vey_	He surveyed the scene.
_des_ert	the Sahara Desert	de_sert_	His wife deserted him.

In some cases the noun can be said to turn into a verb. Indeed the noun _desert_ occurs in English 300 years before the verb. Yet the verb _record_ occurs in the thirteenth century, the noun _record_ a hundred years later, though the modern stress was only fixed in the nineteenth century. The verb _insult_ is recorded in the sixteenth century, the noun _insult_ in the seventeenth century. So, while some nouns may derive from verbs and some verbs derive from nouns, this is often arbitrary; there are simply two alternative forms, one a noun, one a verb, distinguished by their stress. The usual pattern, as seen above, is that nouns and adjectives are stressed on the first syllable (_ex_port, _ab_sent) but verbs are stressed on the second syllable (ex_port_, ab_sent_).

60. Dr. Johnson's Definitions

The first proper dictionary in English is often said to be Samuel Johnson's *Dictionary of the English Language*, published in London in 1755. Some of its definitions of English words are notorious for their idiosyncratic wit; others tell us about eighteenth-century life and show the changes of meaning that words have had since then.

Astrology. The practice of foretelling things by the knowledge of the stars: an art now generally exploded, as without reason.

Cynick. A philosopher of the snarling or currish sort ...

Dull. Not exhilarating; not delightful; as, *to make dictionaries is* dull *work.*

Heathen. Pagan; not Jewish; not Christian.

Ingannation. Cheat ... A word neither used nor necessary.

Itch. A cutaneous disease extremely contagious, which overspreads the body with small pustules filled with a thin serum ... it is cured by sulphur.

Job. (A low word now very much in use, of which I cannot tell the etymology.)

Lass. A girl: a maid ...: used now only of mean girls.

Lesser. A barbarous corruption of *less* ...

Lexicographer. A writer of dictionaries; a harmless drudge.

Macaroon. A coarse rude low fellow ...

Maw-worm. Ordinary gut-worms loosen, and slide off from, the intern tunick of the guts, and frequently creep into the stomach for nutriment being attracted thither by the sweet chyle ...

Mohock. ... ruffians who infested, or rather were imagined to infest, the streets of London.

Network. Any thing reticulated or decussated, at equal distances, with interstices between the intersections.

Oats. A grain, which in England is generally given to horses, but in Scotland supports the people.

Pension. An allowance made to any one without an equivalent. In England it is generally understood to mean pay given to a state hireling for treason to his country.

Pleurisy. Pleurisy is an inflammation of the pleura, though it is hardly distinguishable from an inflammation of any other part of the breast, which are all from the same cause, a stagnated blood; and are to be remedied by evacuation, suppuration or expectoration, or all together.

Politician. A man of artifice; one of deep contrivance.

Sonnet. A short poem consisting of 14 lines ... it is not very suitable to the English language, and has not been used by any man of eminence since Milton.

Tory. (A cant term, derived, I suppose, from an Irish word signifying a savage) ... [Compare the *OED*: "one of the dispossessed Irish, who became outlaws."]

Wolf. A kind of wild dog that devours sheep.

To worm. To deprive a dog of something, nobody knows what, under his tongue, which is said to prevent him, nobody knows why, from running mad.

61. Playing with Words

Many English jokes and witticisms are based on play with words. The teller appears to be using the wrong word but it turns out to make a kind of sense. Oscar Wilde based many of his witticisms on malapropisms (see page 104):

Work is the curse of the drinking classes.
Those whom the gods love grow young.
Moderation is a fatal thing. Nothing succeeds like excess.
Patriotism is the virtue of the vicious.
A true friend stabs you in the front.
Genius is born, not paid.

The humor of Spike Milligan also often depends on deliberate exchanges of similar-sounding words, the kind of mistake we all make accidentally in speech:

After ten days in hospital I took a turn for the nurse.
All men are cremated equal.
Irishman Pat Mebot exploded today after drinking his millionth pint of stout. He is now in the record book of Guinnesses.

Of course some public figures manage to mix up their words without any conscious intention. Take some of the remarks by George W. Bush:

Families is where our nation finds hope, where wings take dream.
He can't take the high horse and then claim the low road.
I just want you to know that, when we talk about war, we're really talking about peace.

62. The Family Tree of English

Most of the languages of Europe belong to the Indo-European family of languages, three exceptions being Basque, Finnish, and Hungarian. This means that they all originated historically from a single hypothetical language called Indo-European. This family includes 449 languages spoken over parts of the world extending from Europe to India – Gaelic, Norwegian, Panjabi, Russian and all the rest – though some are no longer current. Thanks to colonialization and trade, Indo-European languages are now used in every continent, whether Latin America with Spanish or Portuguese, Africa and Canada with French, or Australia with English. The Indo-European family is nevertheless only one out of the 111 language families in the world, which include Sino-Tibetan (403 languages including Chinese) and Basque (3).

The development of Indo-European into the languages spoken today is usually shown in the form of a family tree. Here is a highly pruned tree for languages native to the UK, with the number of languages of each type given in brackets. The four languages still spoken are in bold: English, Welsh, Irish Gaelic, and Scots Gaelic. To them can be added Ulster Scots, spoken by some people in Northern Ireland. The European Union Charter for Regional or

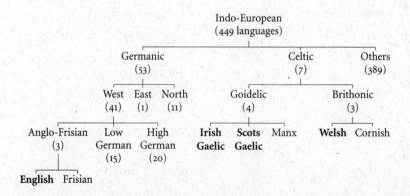

Minority Languages recognizes seven such languages in the UK: Welsh, Scots Gaelic, Irish Gaelic, Scots, Ulster Scots, Cornish, and Manx Gaelic.

Over thousands of years, Indo-European split into eleven branches, two of which are shown here: Germanic and Celtic. Germanic in turn split into three branches, West, East, and North, the North branch leading to the Scandinavian languages such as Norwegian. The West branch split into Anglo-Frisian (Frisia being an area of the eastern shore of the North Sea including Denmark and the Netherlands), Low and High German (Low German leading eventually to Dutch, Swiss German etc.; High German to German and Yiddish). Anglo-Frisian split into English and Frisian.

The indigenous languages of the UK are all related, even if somewhat tenuously. English is closer historically to Dutch and German than to Gaelic or Welsh, reflecting the historical invasions of Anglo-Saxons into England, who drove the people already there to the remoter parts of the west and north.

It is currently debated whether Cornish and Manx are still living spoken languages. Both have fewer than one thousand speakers, who have learned them as heritage languages rather than as their first language, that is to say as part of their heritage giving access to their culture and its literature rather than for everyday use. Klingon, the cult language created for *Star Trek*, is now the most widely used artificial language in the world rather than Esperanto; there is even one baby who learned it as a first language. It now probably has more speakers than Cornish or Manx but, like them, it is learned for cultural rather than for practical reasons.

63. Do You Understand Shakespeare?

People often assume that they understand what Shakespeare's characters say. But the meaning of many Shakespearian words has changed over the past 400 years. Write down what you understand the italicized words in the quotations to mean, then check against the answers on page 285.

1. For *several* virtues have I lik'd several women. THE TEMPEST III/1, 42 ....

2. we of the *offering* side must keep aloof. HENRY IV PART 1 IV/1, 69 ....

3. through all her veins shall run a cold and drowsy *humour.* ROMEO AND JULIET IV/1, 95–6 ....

4. Our *hint* of woe is common. THE TEMPEST II/1, 3–4 ....

5. conference about some *gossips* for your highness. THE WINTER'S TALE II/3, 40–41 ....

6. This is Monsieur Parolles the gallant *militarist.* ALL'S WELL THAT ENDS WELL IV/3, 142 ....

7. Buy food and get thyself in *flesh.* ROMEO AND JULIET V/1, 84 ....

8. thou comest in such a *questionable* state. HAMLET I/4, 43 ....

9. You have a holy father, a *graceful* gentleman. THE WINTER'S TALE V/1, 170–171 ....

10. Horatio and Marcellus, the *rivals* of my watch. HAMLET I/3, 13 ....

11. 'twas caviare to the *general.* HAMLET II/2, 442 ....

12. they are brokers, not of that dye which their *investments* show. HAMLET I/3, 128 ....

13. buckle in a waist most *fathomless.* TROILUS AND CRESSIDA II/2, 30 ....

14. some villain *mountaineers*? I have heard of such. CYMBELINE IV/2, 89–90 ....

In a sense, to understand what Shakespeare's words meant at the time he was writing, we need them to be translated from Elizabethan English to modern English. Of course, each age creates its own Shakespeare; perhaps it does not matter what he meant so much as what we get out of his plays. Modern productions implicitly rely on our modern interpretation of Shakespeare's language, with the exception of a few Shakespearian scholars, and thus superimpose our contemporary meanings on an old text, for good or for ill.

64. A Standard History

The word *standard* seems quite ordinary, a respectable term for keeping standards, speaking standard English, and sticking to the gold standard of A-levels. Yet its history is quite strange.

In 1138 A.D., the English fought the invading Scots at Northallerton in Yorkshire. The English forces rallied round a wagon with the banners of various English dioceses raised on a ship's mast, called a *standard*, i.e. something that stands up, still seen in the modern meaning *standard lamp*. The engagement became known as *The Battle of the Standards*, and so one meaning of *standard* came to be a kind of flag – hence the *Royal Standard*, still flown wherever the Queen of England is in residence. The meaning of "rod or pole" led to *standard* being used from 1429 on to refer to an official measuring rod to guarantee weights and measures, still current in the English *Trading Standards Office*. After 1477 it came to mean "a measure of perfection," more or less the meaning in *standard of living*, etc.

65. Syllables

THE STRUCTURE OF WORDS

Spoken English words are made up of syllables, which have a particular structure of their own in terms of consonants (C) and vowels (V).

The simplest spoken syllable consists of a single vowel (V):

V: *owe, eye, a*

All languages probably have single-vowel syllables. Occasionally a so-called syllabic consonant functions as a whole syllable by itself: the *-on* in *button* and the *-le* in *bottle* are often pronounced as separate syllables with no vowel to be heard.

The next level of complexity is when a spoken syllable consists of a consonant and a vowel (CV):

CV: *tie, key, day*

In some languages, like Japanese, all the syllables are CV; i.e. there are no final consonants, with the exception of nasal consonants like "n." Hence the familiar-looking pattern of Japanese words written in Roman characters, such as *Miyazaki*, *Toyota*, and *Yokahama*, which always seem to end in a vowel.

More complicated still is the spoken syllable that consists of a consonant followed by a vowel and a final consonant (CVC):

CVC: *cat, tip, leaf*

While such syllables are not allowed in Japanese, they are perfectly normal in English.

There are nevertheless restrictions in English on which consonants can begin and end the syllable. A spoken English syllable can't end with an "h" sound – *hat* but not *tah*. Nor can a syllable start with a "ng" sound – *rang* but not *ngar*, though these are possible in other languages. A glance at Chinese names such as *Wong* and *Chen* soon shows that the only consonants allowed at the ends of Chinese syllables are "n" and "ng." The final consonants of English syllables are comparatively varied.

The next level of complexity is how consonants go together to build consonant clusters:

CCVC: *flank* (f + l, n + k); *trots* (t + r, t + s)
CCCVCCC: *strengths* (s + t + r, ng + th + s)

Some clusters, like "fl," can occur at the beginning of a word, *flame*, but others cannot, such as "lf," *lfame*, though that is perfectly possible at the end, as in *self*. "Tn" only exists in Larry Niven's invented species *tnuctipun*. The maximum number of consonants for English is supposed to be three at the beginning of words, like *splinter*, and four at the end, heard in careful enunciation of the ending of *Thou triumphst!*

66. You Silly Politician!
CHANGES OF MEANING

Some words change their meanings slowly, some overnight. *Silly* changed from meaning "innocent," *silly shepherds*, to "stupid," as in *You are silly!*, over hundreds of years. *Gay* on the other hand seems to have acquired the meaning of "homosexual" over a short span in the mid-twentieth century.

There are many ways of classifying these changes of meaning. Examples here are mostly from the *Oxford English Dictionary*, spanning 500 years of English history.

Generalizing: a narrow meaning is extended into a broader one
   cupboard: from "table to put cups on" to "piece of furniture for storage"
   wheels: from "circular revolving objects" to "car" (part for whole)
   have a beer: from "drink a beer" to "go out drinking"
   Hoover: from "vacuum cleaner made by Hoover" to "any vacuum cleaner"
   strange: from "foreign" (*one of the strange Queen's Lords*, Love's Labour's Lost) to "unusual"
   lovely: from "loving" (*a lovely kiss*, 1594) to "nice-looking"
Specializing: a broad meaning is narrowed to a more specific one
   meat: from "food in general," *meat and drink*, to "animal flesh eaten as food"
   deer: from "animal in general" (*mice, and rats, and such small deer*, King Lear) to "ruminant quadruped"
   fowl: from "any kind of bird" (*the fowl of the air*, King James Bible) to "farmyard bird"
   naughty: from "wicked" (*Thou naughty jailor*, 1596) to "mischievous"

complexion: from "temperament" (*suche as be of a hoate complexion*, 1578) to "skin"
Metaphorical: a meaning is extended to something else which is felt to be like it in some way, without the word losing its original meaning
mouse: from "animal" to "computer device"
cool: from "moderately cold" to "classy/sophisticated" (*cool cat*)
tree: from "tall woody plant" to "diagram of a family"

Sometimes the meaning seems to get worse:

cunning: from "learned" (*You must be cunning in the nature of man*, 1637) to "crafty"
cretin: allegedly from "Christian (human being)" in early Romance languages to "idiot"
disease: from "absence of ease" (similar to *ill at ease*) to "morbid physical condition"
to make love: from "to flirt" to "to have sex." In England this transition is sufficiently abrupt that a coursebook for teaching English I used in the 1960s still had sentences using the older meaning (*My boyfriend Cyril made love to me last night*)
gale: from "breeze" (*gentle gales*, 1709) to "violent wind"

Sometimes the meaning seems to get better:

knight: from "lad" to "nobleman"
politician: from "schemer" (*Honest men marry soon, many Politicians not at all*, 1685) to "elected member of a political party"
pretty: from "crafty" (*the prettiest rogue*, 1620) to "attractive"

It is one thing to say how words change; it is quite another matter to explain *why* they change. One obvious cause is that every generation has to assert its differences from its parents; it goes through life as a cohort sharing the same meanings, until its children take up the burden of change. Or the world around us may change: new gadgets need new meanings, whether *mouse* or *computer* (once a person who computes rather than a thing for computing, just as *typewriters*, *printers*, and *drivers* all meant people, not things). Influences come from different sources; UK usage now follows the American meaning of *billion* as "a thousand million" rather than the older UK usage of "a million million" (a trillion in American usage). In the old British sense there are no billionaires in the UK, though there are many in Zimbabwe.

Meanings are still changing rapidly. *Wireless* has gone from meaning "radio" to "unconnected by wires," that is to say from *wireless telephone* to *Wi-Fi*. This does not mean that people do not get annoyed by the shifting sands of vocabulary and see it as some kind of deterioration.

67. Where Do English Words Come From?

THE PUZZLE OF INDO-EUROPEAN

Where did the Indo-Europeans who spoke the language that became English and another 448 languages actually live? Important clues to their original territory come not only from the words that Indo-European languages share, apart from the changes in form that time has subjected them to, but also from the ones that they *don't* share. Indo-European languages often have the same words for "winter" and for "snow"; obviously it was cold where the Indo-Europeans lived. But the languages don't have a common word for "sea," so the Indo-Europeans must have lived inland. The languages share words for "honey," so there must have been bees in the Indo-European homeland. The languages share words for several kinds of farm animals, but not for corn crops, so the Indo-Europeans were nomads rather than farmers. The languages don't have common words for many metals, so Indo-European predates metalworking.

And so on. Of course this argument is not necessarily impeccable. Indo-European languages have common words for "hand" but not for "foot"; obviously the Indo-European had no feet.

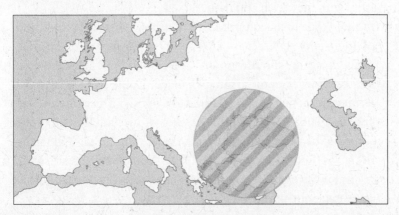

Putting all these clues together suggests an Indo-European homeland somewhere in southeastern Europe around Ukraine and Turkey, as seen on the map. From there, Indo-European marched slowly both west and east.

The precise location of the Indo-European homeland is still hotly disputed. Nevertheless it seems certain that Indo-European languages have a common ancestor somewhere in the shaded region on the map. Recent computer analyses of common vocabulary in ninety-five languages by the evolutionary biologists Russell Gray and Quentin Atkinson suggest that Indo-European started expanding about 7600 B.C. from Anatolia in Turkey.

But why did Indo-European travel across Europe and India in this way? Why should a language spread over vast areas and drive out the languages that are already there? The different explanations that have been put forward come down to:

- *movement of people through migration or conquest.* Groups of people migrated across the face of Europe, wiping out the original inhabitants, just as Celtic languages were pushed to the western and northern fringes of the UK. The non-Indo-European languages Basque and Finnish are, then, surviving pockets of earlier non-Indo-European languages; Hungarian seems to be a later migration. Basque people indeed appear to be genetically distinct from other Europeans, though sharing some characteristics with the Welsh and Irish.
- *farming.* The archaeologist Colin Renfrew correlates the spread of Indo-European across Europe with the spread of farming from Greece in about 6500 B.C., reaching the Orkneys by 3500 BC. As knowledge of farming changed people from hunters to farmers, it carried with it the Indo-European farmers themselves and their language. One piece of supporting evidence is that the spread of bacteria across Europe in early times follows the same route as Indo-European. So Indo-European spread in a common wave of migrant farmers, on Renfrew's calculations at an average rate of one kilometre per year.

• *trade.* The increasing connections between people across Europe meant they needed a common language as a tool, just as people all over the world nowadays learn English as a lingua franca for tourism, business, sport, and so on. If you're going to buy things from or exchange things with other people, you need a language to bargain in.

To the non-specialist in this area, none of these arguments are very convincing. Slow spread at an annual rate is unlike other historical language changes. English spread across other parts of the world in a series of leaps and bounds, say to Australia and Singapore, not gradually. Why would it happen uniformly across all the diverse peoples of Europe? It is difficult enough to get the peoples of Europe to agree on a common agricultural policy, let alone a common language – the EU recognizes twenty-three languages at present.

Conquest and rule by a new elite are unlikely to have replaced one language completely with another. While the ruling classes in England after the Norman Conquest may have used French, English was far from forgotten among the common people and staged a comeback some 300 years later. Total language replacement looks unlikely as an explanation for the spread of Indo-European.

Immigration as a way of importing a new language hardly fits with how immigrants are usually treated; the hosts are not usually eager to learn the immigrants' language but force them to learn theirs, as UK governments still try to do. So far as trade is concerned, most parallels in the modern world involve the inhabitants retaining their original language alongside the lingua franca rather than giving up their first language, as English is used in India. A trade language is a specialized second language, not a replacement for the first language.

The reasons why Indo-European spread so unstoppably remain as mysterious as ever, and perhaps will always stay hidden. There will never be enough concrete evidence of the early pre-history of Europe to show why Indo-European spread other than the sheer fact that it did.

68. Majestic Radiance

SHAKESPEARE'S NEW WORDS

Between 1500 and 1659, 26,947 new words came into English. Around 700 of these are found for the first time in the writings of Shakespeare. This may be coincidence inasmuch as he was using the language of his day along with everybody else who lived in London. He could hardly have peppered his plays with new words without losing the attention of the audience.

Nevertheless, the sheer number of words found for the first time in his plays does suggest that some must have been his own adoption or invention. Many use Latin forms in an un-Latin way, reminding us that, according to Ben Jonson, Shakespeare had "small Latin and less Greek."

Here are some Shakespearean novelties that are still in use today:

abstemious	impair	radiance
accommodation	indistinguishable	refractory
addiction	invulnerable	reinforcement
characterless	invitation	savagery
compulsive	laughable	stricture
consign	majestic	submerge
contentless	mimic	superscript
countless	negotiate	supervise
dateless	obscene	tranquil
deracinate	operate	uncurbed
duellist	overcredulous	undervalue
ensnare	pedant	uneducated
expertness	predecease	unfrequented
fashionable	priceless	unprevailing
fixture	profitless	unquestionable
generous	prophetic	unsolicited
immediacy	proposer	useful

Though they do not necessarily have the same meaning as today, most seem ordinary, the kind of words we couldn't do without for very long. They tend to have several syllables, on a French or Latin model, rather than that of the shorter Old English words.

Saying that Shakespeare was using the language around him does not mean that he did not have a large vocabulary. In his works he uses 31,534 different words. Using a mathematical model, two statisticians, Bradley Efron and Ronald Thisted, calculated that he knew at least another 35,000 that he happened not to use in print, making a total of 66,000 words.

69. Quotations on Words

Definitions

A word is traditionally a "sequence of letters without any spaces."
JAMES HURFORD

A word is an "item listed separately in an ordinary dictionary."
JAMES HURFORD

A word, then, is a form which does not consist of (two or more) lesser free forms; in brief a word is a minimum free form.
LEONARD BLOOMFIELD

A combination of vocal sounds, or one such sound, used in a language to express an idea (e.g. to denote a thing, attribute, or relation), and constituting an ultimate minimal element of speech having a meaning as such; a vocable. *Oxford English Dictionary*

I gotta use words when I talk to you. T. S. ELIOT,
Sweeney Agonistes

Meanings

When *I* use a word ... it means just what I choose it to mean – neither more nor less. LEWIS CARROLL, *Humpty Dumpty*

A word has the meaning someone has given to it.
LUDWIG WITTGENSTEIN

Some words are lonelier than others. J. R. FIRTH

The meaning of words, in law as in life, depends upon their context. MR JUSTICE TUGENDHAT

Aphorisms

People use thought only to justify their wrong-doings, and words only to conceal their thoughts. VOLTAIRE

In the beginning was the Word. *John I.1*

The only sort of four-letter words I use are "good," "love," "warm" and "kind." CATHERINE COOKSON

The world is but a word. SHAKESPEARE, *Timon of Athens*

Ideas are enclosed and almost bound in words like precious stones in a ring. GIACOMO LEOPARDI

Words words words. They're all we have to go on.
TOM STOPPARD, *Rosencrantz and Guildenstern are Dead*

Words are words. I never yet did hear that the bruis'd heart was pierced through the ear. SHAKESPEARE, *Othello*

I am not yet so lost in lexicography as to forget that words are the daughters of earth, and that things are the sons of Heaven.
DR. JOHNSON

All words are prejudices. FRIEDRICH NIETZSCHE

Man does not live by words alone, despite the fact that sometimes he has to eat them. ADLAI STEVENSON

A synonym is a word you use when you can't spell the word you first thought of. BURT BACHARACH

Thus we talk of free enterprise, of capitalist societies ... as though all of these words stand for the same things they formerly did. Social institutions are what they do, not necessarily what we say they do. It is the verb that matters not the noun.
ANEURIN BEVAN

Words are magical in the way they affect the minds of those who use them. ALDOUS HUXLEY

For men converse by means of language; but words are formed at the will of the generality; and there arises from a bad and unapt formation of words a wonderful obstruction to the mind. Nor can the definitions and explanations, with which learned men are wont to guard and protect themselves in some instances, afford a complete remedy: words still manifestly force the understanding, throw every thing into confusion, and lead mankind into vain and innumerable controversies and fallacies.
FRANCIS BACON

There are words which are ugly because of foreignness or ill-breeding (e.g. *television*): but I do not believe that any word well-established in its own language is either beautiful or ugly.
T. S. ELIOT

History teaches that underestimating the words of evil and ambitious men is a terrible mistake. GEORGE W. BUSH

Words will be free; they were born for that. They will seize the brandished weapons of those seeking to enslave them, and will strike the tyrants down. J. M. G. LE CLÉZIO

70. Phrases with Prepositions

A characteristic of English is to combine verbs like *take* with prepositions like *up* to get a new combined expression, *take up*, with a special meaning "to make use of." Or *put* with *up* to get *put up*, "provide accommodation," with *down* to get *put down*, "insult," or with *by* to get *put by*, "save." Or even two prepositions, *put up with*, "endure." The sheer number of different words in the language can be reduced by combining them in distinctive ways, rather like combining the same atoms to make different molecules. Combine *take* with *off*, to get *take off*, "leave the ground," with *in* to get *take in*, "deceive," or with *on* to get *take on*, "hire." And so on with *after*, *down*, *out*, *over*, *up*, and many others.

Even if you know what *take* and *up* mean when they come by themselves, say *He took the bus up the hill*, you can't predict what they mean when they are combined, *He took up the challenge*. Combining verbs and prepositions doesn't just add their meanings together but often creates an entirely new meaning. For this reason, such phrases are often treated as if the combination of preposition and word was a word in its own right and listed separately in dictionaries.

Here are ten uses of *put* with different prepositions, taken from Agatha Christie's *The Mysterious Affair at Styles*. If you look at their meanings, which could be predicted from the combination of the meaning of *put* plus the meaning of the preposition?

1. "He's a great friend of Mary's," *put in* Cynthia.
2. We had just *put away* the last tea-spoon . . .
3. Those of importance we will *put on one side* . . .
4. She was very much *put out* about it.
5. Poirot repeated the question he had *put to* Dorcas . . .
6. He *put* his lips *to* my ear.
7. We have his statement that he *put* the coffee *down* in the hall.

8. Wilkins hadn't an idea of such a thing till Bauerstein *put it into his head.*
9. Did you not *put two and two together* …?
10. She *put off* her project …

To me only 2 and 7 are predictable from the meanings separately.

Such phrases are an enormous problem for people learning English, whether children learning their first language or students learning their second; you can't just acquire the meanings of single words in isolation but have to learn the combinations of words with prepositions as if they were words with a meaning of their own. The size of your vocabulary is not just how many words you know, but how many word combinations.

71. What is a Word?

It seems perfectly obvious what a word is: *beer* is a word, *reeb* is not; *beer* has a meaning, *reeb* does not. So a word is a sequence of letters (or sounds) with meaning. Is that all there is to it?

For over a hundred years linguists have found it handy to talk also about morphemes – the smallest elements of language that have meaning. Sometimes a morpheme may be a word: *beer* is a morpheme as it has a meaning, *reeb* is not a morpheme as it has no meaning – it's a nonsense word. Sometimes a morpheme may be smaller than a word: *beers* and *beery* have different meanings from *beer*, so the elements *-s* and *-y* count as morphemes, as they have meanings but are not words. The idea of the morpheme is then a useful complement to the idea of the word.

So what is a word? Some of the alternatives are:

• *words are units that are able to occur on their own*
What makes *beer* a word is that you can say it on its own rather than having to put it with other words:

What'll you have?
Beer.

But the morphemes *-s* and *-y* need a word to cling to, *beers/beery*, *flours/floury* etc., rather than being said on their own. It is hard to think of sensible questions to which *-s* and *-y* are possible answers (except in technical discussions of language).

Did he write a novel?
s. [i.e. more than one?]

Is it beer?

y. [like beer, but not actually beer?]

One working definition of "word" is therefore the smallest unit of language that can be said on its own: *beer* is a word; *y* is not. We can call *-s* and *-y* "bound" morphemes, as opposed to "free" morphemes like *black* and *cheer*, as they are bound to a word, just like *-ish*, *blackish*, or *-ly*, *cheerily*. Words, then, are "free" morphemes. But it would be very hard to compile a dictionary by hunting for occasions on which every word occurred on its own rather than as part of a sentence. Nor does this definition include the important category of structure words like *of* and *my*, which cannot occur on their own, yet are clearly words.

- *words are chunks that can't be split up*
  In English you can add bits to the beginning of a word, *happy* > *unhappy*, by adding the bound morpheme *un-*; or to the end, *happy* > *happiness*, by adding the bound morpheme *-ness*. But you usually can't put them in the middle; a word can't be interrupted. The only exceptions are a handful of exclamations such as *absobloominglutely*, where *blooming* comes in the middle of *absolutely*, and Homer Simpson's *saxamophone*. While the definition that words can't be interrupted works well for English, it doesn't work at all for languages that thrive on building up words internally, like Inuit languages.

- *words are items listed in a dictionary*
  A word is also something that is listed in a dictionary: you can look up the word *beer* but you can't look up the morpheme *-s* (though it does depend on the dictionary, some of which will certainly have an entry for the meanings of *-y*). When we talk about the words of a language, it is usually this dictionary list that we have in mind.

  There are still problems. Dictionaries actually have "entries" rather than words. *Man* is one entry, hence it is one word. But this does not mean that it has only one meaning; the *Oxford English Dictionary* (*OED*) has seventeen main meanings for *man* as a noun, including the expected "a human being (irrespective of sex or age)" but also "one of the pieces used in chess" and "a cairn or pile of stones marking a summit or prominent point of a mountain." If the principle is one word = one meaning, how many words *man* are there? The list of separate entries in the dictionary gives only a rough guide to the numbers of words without counting the meanings.

Sometimes these multiple meanings are treated as homophones – different words with the same pronunciation but different meanings, like *right* (correct), *rite* (ritual), *write* (to make written symbols) and *Wright* (a surname). (Incidentally, this shows that a bonus of the English spelling system is that writing clearly distinguishes between words that sound the same in speech.) Sometimes the multiple meanings are seen as extensions from a "central meaning." The central meaning of "human being" for *man* extends to anything that looks like a human being, such as a cairn of stones. Again the definition of words as items on a list is not totally satisfactory.

- *words are chunks divided by spaces or sounds*
  A word is also a chunk of language that can be chopped out of a sentence. Speakers can separate the words out of the stream of speech with clear pauses: *We – shall – overcome*. But this word-by-word style of speaking is normally heard only from beginning readers and Daleks. Instead we tend to run spoken words together. It is hard to detect pauses in between the words when listening to someone speaking – *weshallovercome*. Listen to a language you don't know and you have little idea where words begin and end. In speech, pauses are used to show grammatical divisions, hesitations, and so on, rarely divisions between words. So pauses are potential clues to words even if this possibility is seldom used in speech.

Written words are very different. English words stand out because they have spaces in between them. We know that there are three words in *We shall overcome* because of the spaces: a word is "a sequence of letters without any spaces." This simple definition works well for written English and certainly solves the problem of distinguishing between words and morphemes, which are not necessarily separated by spaces. The most popular working definition is undoubtedly: if it has a space before it and a space after it, it's a word.

The convention of putting spaces between words only came in around the eighth century A.D.; English had gotten along without it for several centuries. Did Old English therefore not have words? Nor does it apply to other languages. Chinese has spaces between characters, not between words; Thai and Inuit are alphabetic scripts like English but see no need to separate words with spaces. If words need spaces, then none of these languages has words. Defining spoken language on the basis of written words puts the cart before the horse. Most linguists insist that speech is more basic than writing and that therefore it is illogical to base the definition of a spoken word on the written language.

Having sorted out where words start and end, we still have problems with what counts as a word in English. *Carpet* is a word and fits all the above definitions. So is *carpets* a different word because it has a plural *-s*? Is *to carpet* a different word because it's a verb? A *carpeter*? Are *carpeting* and *carpeted* still more words? But what about *recarpet* and *uncarpeted*? *Carpet bag* and *red-carpet*? Does counting the number of occurrences of *carpet* in English texts mean adding up all of these nouns, verbs, and adjectives, and so on, or counting each one separately? Do we draw the line at compound words like *red carpet*? Or are we even stricter, excluding forms that have added morphemes like *carpeter* or *recarpet*? Indeed, I thought I had made these two words up – the spell-checker in Word rejected them – until I checked on Google and found 9,000 Web pages with *carpeter* and

20,000 with *recarpet*. This shows how difficult it is to set a figure on how many words someone knows or how many words there are in a language: it all depends on what counts as a word. The reason why dictionaries differ in the words they list is that they use different rules for working out what a word is.

One solution is to count not words but word families. A word family is defined by the vocabulary specialist Paul Nation as "a headword, its inflected forms, and its closely related derived forms." Included with the headword *book* as a noun are the inflected form *books* and the derived form *bookish*; *book* as a verb has the inflected forms *books*, *booked*, and *booking*, and the derived forms *bookable* and *booker*. So there are two *book* families of words, nouns and verbs.

But is *booklet* part of the noun family *book*? A *bookie* part of the verb family *book*? Each person comes to a different decision – before you even ponder whether elements in a word family have to share a common meaning – is the *book* which is a "printed treatise" in the same family as the *book* in "words to which a musical is set"? Or "the total of charges against a person" or "a record of bets"? And the meaning affects which of the related forms can be used: *bookish* can't be used for musicals; *bookies* take bets but *bookers* book tickets.

72. One English or Many Englishes?

English has become a world language spoken in countries ranging from Canada to India to Australia. An ongoing battle concerns the status of local versions of English in particular countries. Must they stay as close as possible to standard British or American, or can they assert language independence as well as political independence? Is it as right for an Indian to speak Indian English as it is for an English person to speak British English?

Here are some words from particular local Englishes. Some are borrowed from local languages; others may be English words but have rather different meanings from American English. It's only the outsider that finds this a problem. All of them work perfectly well for their own speakers in their own area.

Indian English words

batchmate	classmate
by-two coffee	one portion of coffee divided between two customers
co-brother	wife's sister's husband
eve-teasing	teasing young women
finger chips	chips
hotel	restaurant only (i.e. no guest rooms, sometimes found in England)
keybunch	bunch of keys
meeting notice	notice of a meeting
policewallah	policeman (and many other kinds of *wallah*)
stepney	spare wheel

Singapore English words

chope	to reserve
Do you take hot food?	Do you like hot food?
kuku house	asylum

makan	food
more better	better
to open a light	to turn on (a light)
uncle	middle-aged man

West African English words

been-to	a person who has been to England
carpet	linoleum
hot drink	alcoholic drink
outside child (Liberia)	a child born out of wedlock
to bluff (Sierra Leone)	to be elegantly dressed
to have long legs (Ghana)	to have influence

In these countries English is an official language, and we can speak of a local standard English, even if the inhabitants themselves often prefer not to acknowledge it. Sometimes these local Englishes are labelled with a term ending in *-lish*. So Singapore English is referred to as *Singlish* and has its own quirks, such as ending sentences with *lah*: *You like her, lah?*

However, the *-lish* ending also refers to deviations from standard English as well as locally acceptable varieties. *Japlish*, for example, consists of odd uses of English in Japan, such as:

Coffee. Relax and have a nice coffeebreak. So you can meet the something wonderful happen.

Or:

REVOLTING FASHION FOR MEN

Before the 2008 Olympics, the Chinese authorities were worried that *Chinglish* notices, such as *Collecting money toilet*, would confuse foreign visitors to Beijing. In the United States people talk about *Spanglish*, the variety used by Spanish-speaking immigrants; in Korea about *Konglish*. In this case the varieties of English called *-lish* are not acceptable local variants but full of accidental mistakes.

A third type of -lish refers to a problem for e-mail users whose languages do not use a Roman script. In an ideal world, all computers would be set up to handle all scripts without favoring any of them. But often you cannot guarantee that the person you are writing to can read your message in the Greek script, Arabic and so on. So, quite spontaneously, people have invented ways of converting other scripts into Roman. Greeks send their emails in something called *Greeklish* – Greek spelled in Roman letters – by looking for Roman letters or numbers that resemble Greek. Users of Arabic, Russian, and Chinese scripts have also spontaneously invented ways of using Roman script in this informal way. Cinema posters in Egypt are written in both normal Arabic and "Latinized" Arabic. Since the language used in English texting contains many of these devices, it could be called *Englishlish*.

So Singlish, Spanglish, and Greeklish are very different types of -lish. Each of these varieties of English is disapproved of by various groups. The British may disapprove of Indian English as they think British English is the only valid form. The Singapore government frowns on Singlish because it is not standard English. Some Greeks scorn Greeklish because they say it is destroying the Greek language. Russians call their Romanized script *Volapuk* – taken from the name of an artificial language like Esperanto because of its weird appearance. Varieties of language are always tied into people's identities and communities.

73. From TLV to IKA

ABBREVIATIONS FOR AIRPORTS

If you were a luggage sorter at an airport, where would you send bags with these labels? Answers on page 286.

Part 1 internal (within the U.S.)

1. LAX .... 2. EWR .... 3. IAH ....

4. ITO .... 5. MDW ....

Part 2 short haul (all in Europe)

1. MRS .... 2. BUD .... 3. ZYD ....

4. FCO .... 5. SOF ....

Part 3 long haul (outside Europe)

1. HKG .... 2. TPE .... 3. NRT ....

4. CCS .... 5. TLV ....

The official three-letter airport code laid down by IATA accommodates all the airports of the world. The basic system takes letters from the spelling of the destination, sometimes just the first three, as in BUD (Budapest), sometimes spread through the word, as in MRS (Marseilles), sometimes only initial letters, as in LGW (London Gatwick).

This is not helpful to travelers when the inhabitants use a local name like STN (Stansted, a village some way outside London) or FCO (Fiumicino, a seaside town near Rome; the airport is also known as Leonardo da Vinci). The initials are, however, sometimes more helpful than the actual name of the airport, unless you are well up on the names of local heroes: HAV (José Marti, Havana), JFK (John F. Kennedy, New York), CCS (Simón Bolívar, Carácas), TPE (formerly Chiang Kai-Shek, Taipei), IKA (Imam Khomeini Airport, Tehran).

74. Word Games with Sequences

Sequence games create chains of words or sentences based on different ways in which a word given by one player can be related to a word from another player.

- in **word association** games, each player has to produce a word related in meaning to the previous player's: *sky, plane, pollution* … etc. Players are eliminated if they dry up or produce a word that has no discernible relation to the previous word. Examples of some typical word associations are on page 99.

- in **alphabetic sequence** games, players have to produce a word beginning with the next letter of the alphabet, as in the game known as *The Parson's Cat*:

The parson's cat is an angry cat.
The parson's cat is a bashful cat.
The parson's cat is a clever cat …

A player who can't think of an appropriate word is eliminated or loses a life. These alphabet games are sometimes played without the letters *X, Y,* and *Z* as they provide too limited a range of words to choose from.

   An alternative way of going through the alphabet is *I Love My Love,* in which a series of statements about your love rotates through the letters of the alphabet:

I love my love with an A because she is awesome.
I hate her with an A because she is ambitious.
Her name is Anne and she comes from Aldeburgh.

And so on for the Bs, etc.

   The sequence can also depend on the last letter of the word. Players have to choose a category such as "countries" and then make each country start with the letter the previous one ended in:

Canada
Afghanistan
New Zealand ...

- **structured sequence games** involve predetermined sequences of moves or sentences. A well-known joke version is Humphrey Lyttelton's *Mornington Crescent*, in which players complete a journey round London based on never-stated sequencing rules.

  In the traditional game of *Consequences* players produce a story collectively. This was popular with Victorians, possibly on account of the slightly risqué combinations it easily produces. Players build up a story by writing words on pieces of paper which they pass round a circle each turn, having folded them over to conceal what they have written. One of the many variants has six turns:

  1. (man's name) .... met
  2. (woman's name) ....
  3. in the (place name) ....
  4. He said to her: " .... "
  5. She said to him: " .... "
  6. And the consequence was: ....

  But the skeleton story can easily be amplified as much as the players like by asking for adjectives for the nouns, finishing with "And the world said ' .... ,'" and adding extra elements to the story skeleton.

- **in a word sequence game** a large group of players improvise a story by adding one word at a time in rotation, a sort of uncontrolled *Consequences*.

75. Can You Talk Black?

This test measures outsiders' knowledge of Black American English. Answers are on page 287.

1. Who is the baddest man in America? ....
2. Is it good for a woman to be womanish? ....
3. What do you do when you're mobbin'? ....
4. When are you DWB? ....
5. Have you committed a sin if you're "evil"? ....
6. Is it good to be straight? ....
7. When does the eagle fly? ....
8. Who might be your big momma? ....
9. When would you get your clown off? ....
10. If you pimp another person in a match, do you win or lose? ....
11. If someone has a chocolate jones, are they allergic to it? ....
12. Where is the Promised Land? ....
13. Is it good for a child to be grown? ....
14. Would you git happy in church? ....
15. Are crips good for you? ....
16. When are you in the system? ....
17. Would you wear a silk? ....
18. Is your hair relaxed? ....
19. Who is a brotha? ....
20. Would you be juiced if you won a million pounds? ....

If the test seems hard to someone who is not a black American, imagine how a black American child feels coping with standard American English. In other words, a test of language has to measure people on the kind of language *they* speak, not the language of some other group. It puts black children at a disadvantage if they are measured by tests of white language, working-class people by middle-class standards, or bilinguals by monolingual native speakers. It is not surprising these speakers are thought to have language problems if they are not being tested on their own variety of language.

The idea for this test came from a test called the *Bitch 100*, which showed that white Americans could not speak black English, so why should black children have to speak white English?

76. Place Names around the English-speaking World

Place names in English-speaking countries often rely on natural features and the people who lived there but also draw on indigenous languages, the history of colonialism, and the colonists' homesickness.

Canada

The names of Canadian cities show a range of influences not just from the official languages, English and French, but also from native Canadian languages.

Toronto: comes from Mohawk *tkaronto*, meaning either literally "where there are trees standing in the water" or less literally "fishing weirs"; from 1793 to 1834 it was called *York* after the English town.

Quebec: from an Amerindian word *kebek*, meaning "a strait"

Halifax: named after the Earl of Halifax, 1716–71

New Brunswick: when it was partitioned from Nova Scotia in 1784, it was named after the House of Brunswick in honor of King George III.

USA

American names also reflect local languages, colonial languages, links to political figures, and nostalgia for home.

St. Louis, Louisiana, Louisville: named after various King Louis of France

New Orleans: named after the Duke of Orléans

Des Moines: from French Rivière des Moines (Monks' River)

Montana: from Spanish montaña (mountain)

Florida: from Spanish florida, both because it is covered in flowers and because it was discovered during Pasqua Florida (the flower festival shortly after Easter)

New Zealand

Auckland: named after the first Earl of Auckland, 1840
Canterbury: named after the English town
Rotorua: based on "Second Lake" (or rather "Lake Second") in Maori

The four most copied names from England globally, according to a list from the London *Times*, are *Richmond*, *London*, *Oxford*, and *Manchester*.

77. Children's Mistakes

Children's mistakes tell us something about how they are learning to speak. Here are some types of mistakes that American children make, as described by J. J. Jaeger.

- *saying one content word rather than another* – only true of course if both words are in their current vocabulary:

  Which one's the Bambi? No, which one's the baby?
  (age 3 years: 4 months)

  Grandma Beckie lives in Husted … Houston (5:7)

  This kind of mistake is quite common in adult speech. Immediately after saying a word, we recognize that it's the wrong one and correct it. The fact that the mistake is similar in pronunciation or in meaning to the right word shows how words are linked in our minds.

- *saying one structure word rather than another*:

  She doesn't like his brother – I mean her brother. (5:1)

  I need to put it under … over my shirt. (2:11)

  Again, this is quite common in adults. Out of a limited choice of words, such as pronouns (*her/his*) or opposites (*under/over*), we choose the wrong one.

- *blending words*, making a new word by combining two existing words:

  I've get a spork (3:7) (spoon/fork)

  I'm going to gobble up all my pumpcorn (4:5) (pumpkin/popcorn)

This is a common way of forming new words in English, as seen on page 42, and children do it as much as anyone.

- *anticipating*, saying a word that should have come later in the sentence:

  Ali put her mouth over ... Ali put her hand over her mouth. (4:10)

  We're gooding ... we're doing good. (5:7)

  The phrase *hand over mouth* has been assembled out of the right words but they have not been put in the right sequence.

- *perseverating*, repeating a word that should have come earlier in the sentence:

  That might be go in there. (4:9)

  Daddy, me watching Daddy cooking ... no ... Mommy's cooking. (2:4)

- *spoonerisms*, swapping words or parts of words:

  Her run is nosing. (2:7)

  I get glumpy ... grumpy when I sleep. (3:3)

  This is a common process in adult speech, described on page 118.

- *swapping adjacent words around*:

  I'm not that in big of a hurry. (4:5)

  They're not either home ... they're not home either. (4:2)

  Another sign of the stages of speaking getting muddled: the words are there but the ordering isn't.

78. Four Hundred and Thirty Sets

The longest entry for a word in the *Oxford English Dictionary* is for the verb *set*, which has more than 430 senses, divided into 154 main sections – effectively a book of 60,000 words in itself. Ordinary meanings include:

- *to descend:* the sun set in the west
- *to put in a definite place:* he set the table
- *to ordain something:* they set the rules of engagement

But how about more specific meanings?

- she was set in her ways
- the jelly set
- he set him up for the knockout
- the ring was set with diamonds
- something set him apart from the crowd
- he set the time on his watch
- she set her latest novel in Greece

All of these – and most of the other 400-odd meanings – would be understood by any English speaker, a mammoth amount of information about one word.

79. Baby Talk across Languages

Baby talk is the term for how some parents adapt their speech to small babies because they feel it makes it easier for them to understand, not for the language the babies use themselves. The words of baby talk are quite similar in different languages:

mother: *mummy/mum/mom/ma* (English), *mama* (Arabic, Swahili, Greek), *maman* (French), *mutti* (German), *ma* (Berber)
cow: *moo cow* (English), *moo* (Swahili), *moomoo* (Japanese)
dog: *bow-wow* (English), *wan wan* (Japanese), *myow* (Arabic), *toutou* (French), *vau vau* (Latvian), *haw-haw* (Arabic), *waw-waw* (Greek)
stomach: *tummy* (English), *pompon* (Japanese), *umbo* (Swahili), *bumbuls* (Latvian)

Baby talk words imitate actual sounds, which people apparently hear slightly differently in various parts of the world, unless of course dogs actually bark differently in Latvia and Japan. They also show a universal tendency to repeat the same syllable (*moomoo*) or to repeat it with a different first sound (*bow-wow*).

See if you can work out what these baby talk words refer to in various languages. Answers on page 288:

1. *kong kong* ....

2. *nyannyan* ....

3. *kuku* ....

4. *dadush* ....

5. *lalalal* ....

6. *shii shii-shii-sura* ....

7. *peton* ....

80. Night Night Moo

CHILDREN'S EARLY WORDS

Children's early words are significant events for many parents. Here is a timeline showing when 50 percent of children say a particular word, based on U.S. children. As this is an average, there is no reason to be pleased or disappointed if a particular child is a bit earlier or later than the point on the timeline. Each child has his or her own pattern of acquisition, speeding up or slowing down at different ages.

Months	Words
12	daddy, mommy
13	bye
14	dog, hi
15	baby, ball, no
16	banana, eye, nose, bottle, juice, bird, duck, cookie, woof, moo, ouch, baabaaa, night night, book, balloon, boat
17	cracker, apple, cheese, ear, keys, bath, peekaboo, vroom, up, down
18	grandma, grandpa, sock, hat, truck, boat, thank you, cat

Early words tend to fall into particular types, such as:

- people: *daddy, grandma, baby*
- animals: *cat, bird, dog*
- toys: *ball, balloon*

The timeline demonstrates how children's vocabulary starts exploding when they are around sixteen months, known as the "vocabulary spurt."

81. Ept and Chalant

BACK-FORMED WORDS

Some English words were originally formed by adding a prefix to another word, even before the word actually reached English. *Decide, insist, persuade* all existed in Latin complete with *de, in* and *per*, along with *desist, persist, dissuade* and so on. Sometimes the original word no longer exists in modern English – what is the *sheveled* in *disheveled*, for instance? (It was once to do with the French *cheveux*, meaning "hair.") Or the *abashed* in *unabashed* (last met in Tennyson in 1859: "Enid, all abash'd she knew not why…")?

A minor fad in the twentieth century was to reinvent the original form of the word by detaching the prefix, called "back-formation." So in the film *Born Yesterday* a character back-forms *couth* from *uncouth*: "I'm every bit as couth as you are!" and in *The Code of the Woosters* P. G. Wodehouse invents *gruntled* from *disgruntled*, "If not actually disgruntled, he was far from being gruntled." These seem to be humorous one-offs, even if online dictionaries regard them as normal words. They may nevertheless survive in some local dialects.

In a *New Yorker* piece, "How I Met My Wife," Jack Winter takes it to the logical limit by back-forming words with:

un: wieldy, gainly, requited
in: consolate, terminable, ept
non: plussed, chalant, descript
im: peccable, maculate, petuous
dis: concerting, array, may
mis: givings, nomer

82. More Up

CHILDREN'S TWO-WORD COMBINATIONS

In the 1960s, the psychologist Martin Braine had the insight that young children's word combinations follow a set of rules of their own rather than those of adult language. Here are some of the two-word phrases that he analyzed, produced by an American boy named Andrew when he was nearly two years old.

all broke	more car	airplane by
all buttoned	more fish	siren by
all clean	more high	
all done	more hot	no bed
all dressed	more read	no down
all fix	more sing	no fix
all gone	more walk	no pee
all messy		no wet
all through	see baby	
all shut	see pretty	mail come
all wet	see train	mama come

Braine recognized two types of words in Andrew's speech. One type were "open" words like *walk* or *wet* that occurred freely on their own. The other type were "pivot" words like *more* or *all* that could not occur by themselves but had to be accompanied by an open word, as in *more fish* and *all shut*. So the child's two-word sentences are made up of a pivot word and an open word, in some ways resembling the adult division between content words like *walk* and structure words like *to* (see page 33). Sometimes the pivot word comes first in the child's sentence, like *no* in *no wet* or *see* in *see baby*; sometimes second, like *by* in *airplane by* and *come* in *mail come*. The child's rule for forming two-word sentences is therefore:

combine a pivot word with an open word. This is a far cry from the complex rules that adults use to make sentences but this simple rule is nevertheless followed consistently by the child. The child's sentence may be something an adult could never say. Nevertheless it is perfectly logical in the child's own terms: *no wet, more high, see pretty, siren by*.

Some children's early sentences don't fit this pivot/open rule, such as the following examples from Andrew:

airplane all gone	what's that	pants change
all done milk	mail man	dry pants
byebye back	our car	up on there
papa byebye	our door	off bib

While this pivot/open analysis of children's two-word sentences works quite well, Braine himself and later researchers have turned to more complex analyses. One reason is that it explains only the actual combination of words, not what the child means.For example, *more car* might be a request to hand over another model car, *more hot* a request to turn the heating up. In a famous example, a child was heard saying *mommy sock* with different meanings on two occasions, once to say that the sock belonged to mommy, once to request that mommy put her sock on. Just treating two-word combinations as pivot and open may conceal some of what the child is doing with language.

83. Brown Blackbirds and Black Bluebottles

COMPOUND WORDS

When two words are added together to get a new word, they form a compound. Sometimes it is a matter of adding the meaning of the two words: a *madman* is a man who is mad. Usually the meaning of the compound word is more than the sum of its parts. You would be wrong if you guessed that a *sheepdog* is a dog that looks like a sheep, or that an *electric chair* is a wheelchair with a motor.

The links between the two words in compounds are diverse. Here are some possibilities:

- *blackberry* (a particular type of *berry* that is *black*), *highchair* (a particular kind of *chair* that is *high*): the first word is an adjective that adds to the meaning of the noun
- *heartbreak* (the state of a *heart* that *breaks*), *snakebite* (when a *snake* has *bitten* someone), *cloudburst* (a storm like a *cloud bursting*): the first word is the subject of the following verb
- *watchmaker* (a person who *makes watches*); *bookseller* (a person who *sells books*): the first word acts as the object of the following verb with *-er* added
- *fishing rod* (a *rod* for *fishing*), *ironing board* (*board* for *ironing*), *carving knife* (a *knife* that *carves*): the first word carries out the action of the second

But there are many other ways of making compounds. Just sticking to *dog*, we find:

- a *lapdog* (a dog that sits on a lap, sometimes used metaphorically)

- a *puppydog* (a dog that is a puppy)
- *a bulldog* (a dog that is like a bull)
- a *sheepdog* (a dog that herds sheep)
- a *police dog* (a dog used by the police)
- a *watchdog* (a dog that watches, with metaphorical uses)
- a *hunting dog* (a dog used for hunting)
- a *lazy dog* (a person who is lazy)

Often there are two alternative forms, one a compound, one a simple combination. Take colors:

a white board/a whiteboard	*the white house/the White House*
a black bird/a blackbird	*a black berry/a blackberry*
a blue bottle/a bluebottle	*an Orangeman/an orange man*
a blue tooth/Bluetooth	*a black bottom/the blackbottom*
a black shirt/a blackshirt	*a red admiral/a Red Admiral*
a red neck/a redneck	*a green house/a greenhouse*
a red cap/a redcap	*a yellow jacket/a yellowjacket*

So it is possible to get contradictory phrases such as *a brown blackbird, a black bluebottle, a low highchair* or an advertisement for a porn shop, *blue movies in full color.*

Spelling and hyphenation are not usually good guides to whether a word is a compound. Sometimes there is a space between the words of a compound (*The White House*); sometimes a hyphen (*tea-time*); sometimes neither (*blackberry*). The longer the word has been in English the more likely it is to have lost its space and its hyphen. The *Oxford English Dictionary* records a progression from *tea bag* (1898) to *tea-bag* (1936) to *teabag* (1977).

Pronunciation gives a better clue, since compounds tend to be stressed on the first word, like *the White House*, and non-compounds to have even stress on both words, as in *the white house*. A famous example for linguists is *the lighthouse* versus *the light house* or, even better, *the lighthouse keeper* versus *the light house-keeper*.

Children get the knack of inventing new compounds very early on. A child studied by the psycholinguist Eve Clark produced *baby-milk* (21 months), *bubble-hair* (22 months), *Babar-book* (23 months), *orange-juice-box* (2 years, 1 month) and *boat-shirt* (2 years, 3 months).

84. How Do Children Learn Words?

How do children actually learn words? While the facts of children's language development are fairly well known, it is still far from clear just how they learn them.

First, there is the size of the problem. Adults know enormousnumbers of words. The size of people's vocabularies has proved hard to estimate. The psychologist Paul Bloom estimates that seventeen-year-olds know 60,000 actual words. Looking backward at what they have achieved, this means that, ignoring the first year of life, they have learned 3,750 words a year, or about ten a day. Three-year-olds are managing only about ten words a week; older children must be absorbing new words at a considerably higher rate.

The graph below shows the average number of words learned by a child each day.

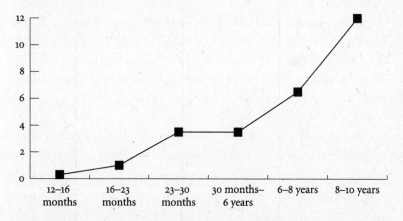

As adults we are still taking in new words all the time, not only through exposure to words we have never happened to encounter before, in, for instance, the terminology of a new subject one gets interested in, whether soccer, in which one might find *Catenaccio* (a defensive system), or architecture, where one might find

Palladian (a particular style), but also through the new words coming into the language, such as *iPhone* and *coronavirus*.

The traditional common-sense belief is that a child learns a word by associating the word with a visible object. A mother points to a dog and says *A Doggie!* and the child associates the word with the object itself. Next time she sees it, the child can say *doggie*, to her parents' delight. In some sense this explanation must be true. Words in our minds are linked to visible objects and events in the world: I can point to a bird flying and say *flying*. But this doesn't work with things that cannot be seen; *I know that* – how do you point to an action of knowing? How do you see the object known as *air*?

Philosophers have shown a logical problem with associating words with things by pointing to them and naming them: how do you know which aspect of the world is the thing the word is associated with? That is to say, how do you know exactly what it *is* that someone is pointing to? Most of the things in the world have many features. A tennis ball has a color (yellow), a material (rubber), a shape (spherical), a purpose (it's for tennis), an age (new or worn out), and other characteristics (bouncy, breaks windows, etc.). If someone who spoke another language pointed to a tennis ball and said *Shradditch*, how would you know which of these attributes he actually meant? It could be the name for the ball, it could be the color, it could be anything else at all that the speaker wanted to say.

The child has therefore to work out which aspect of the world goes with the word. The world is not conveniently divided up into objects with single features. Naming means being able to sort out which aspect of a thing is being named.

Not even the fondest of parents actually spend much time labeling things – *Look, Jimmy, a train!* Instead, they do more complicated things like describing the train – *What a nice train!* – or warning – *Watch out! The train's coming!* – or complaining – *The train's late again.* We don't often say *That's a train*, because it would be such a boringly obvious thing to say.

A story told among linguists concerns a researcher who was studying a previously unknown language spoken by a remote tribe. To find out the words of the language, he got people from the tribe to sit down on the other side of a table one at a time. He started by pointing at the table and saying *Table*. The first tribesman nodded vigorously and said something which the researcher dutifully wrote down. When he did the same with the next tribesman, the answer was a different word. And the third and fourth tribesman produced still different words. *Wonderful!*, thought the linguist. *A language with four different words for "table"!* Only much later did he discover that the first tribesman had said *Wood*, the next, *You're pointing*, the third, *Table*, the fourth, *I don't know*, all showing their interpretations of what was going on in the situation, only one of which corresponded to his version. In other words, it was far from obvious which word went with *table*, except in the eye of the researcher.

The same with children. When the mother says *milk*, she might be referring to the bottle the milk is in or to the act of giving the child a drink. If someone points to a red ball in a picture and says *Red*, what can the child get out of it? *Red* might be a word for the ball itself, or a word for a round shape, or a word for a picture, and doubtless there are other interpretations. The child must have a way of working out which of the possible meanings the adult is using.

The philosopher Willard Quine put it in terms of hearing someone who speaks another language say *Gavagai*, as a rabbit scurries by. *Gavagai* might be a word for "rabbit" in general, or it might be the pet name of an individual rabbit. Or it could mean "one for the pot." Or it could describe any aspect of the rabbit (furry, white, big, etc.). Or any part of the rabbit – nose, legs, etc. The problem with learning how words go with things we see is sorting out which aspects of what we see are important and which are irrelevant.

Modern language teachers face the same problem of conveying what new words mean to their students. A fashionable teaching method a few years ago was audiovisualism. This meant showing students pictures and giving them language to associate with them: a picture of a car and the French word *l'auto*; a picture of a smiling face and the French *bonjour*. Often this failed to work because the students did not interpret the pictures in the way the teacher wanted. They saw the car as a sedan or an old jalopy rather than just a car. I once observed a primary-school teacher explaining the word *car* to second language children in London. Following the lesson, the children had to count traffic on the street, so I pointed to a car and said to a boy, *What's that?* He answered, *That's a Ford. My father drives a Jag.* He hardly needed a picture to learn the word *car*. A smiling face in a picture could mean almost anything; in many cultures smiling is a sign of embarrassment rather than friendliness. The audiovisual method works well enough for words whose meanings can be demonstrated visually, but not for abstract words, structure words or many others. It relies on everybody solving Quine's problem in the same way by having the same interpretation of the picture.

So, when children meet a new word, how do they know which of the umpteen different possibilities for its meaning is right? Children might play it safe by waiting for the next time they hear *gavagai*: if it's said when there are lots of rabbits about in different colors, that eliminates the color meaning, if the next time it is said the rabbit in question is obviously no longer edible, that eliminates "one for the pot." And so on until the child gets the right meaning. But this puts an enormous burden on children's memory and language-learning processes. They'd have to store, say, ten memories of the word along with the details of each situation before they got the meaning. And this would be happening for 3,750 new words a year, i.e. 37,500 memories.

The psychologist Lawrence W. Barsalou claims that this is indeed more or less how we learn vocabulary. A word is remembered in combination with the situation in which we learned it rather than its meaning getting detached; its meaning is distributed around different parts of the mind rather than being stored as a single item. When people think of the word *sky*, their eyes often actually move upward. Think of the word *run*; the areas that are activated in your brain are those not just for vocabulary but also for movement. In our minds, words go along with situations. Activating a word brings up everything else in our mind that goes with it. Hence athletes with an injury can gain from practising mentally what they cannot do physically.

The psychologist Michael Tomasello showed that to learn a word, you did not even need to see the object it refers to. An adult looks for a *gazzer* in four boxes. Three of them reveal ordinary toys for which the child knows the words. The fourth is locked and the adult pretends to be frustrated by not being able to find the *gazzer*, shaking it to hear something rattle inside. Later the child is shown the three toys together with another new toy, for which he or she does not have a name, and is asked to choose the *gazzer*. By picking it out correctly, children show that they have learned a word for something they had never seen by working it out from the adult's behavior. It is not just associating words with things that is important; it is knowing what naming an object means.

85. Choosing Words for Reading

In the United Kingdom, the National Curriculum (1999) lays down these word lists for children to read at different ages.

First year
I, go, come, went, up, day, was, look, are, the, of, we, this, do, me, like, going, big, she, and, they, my, see, on, away, Mum, it, at, play, no, yes, for, a, Dad, can, he, am, all, is, cat, get, said, to, in

Year 1 to 2
about, can't, her, many, over, then, who, after, could, here, may, people, there, will, again, did, him, more, push, these, with, an, do, his, much, pull, three, would, another, don't, home, must, put, time, your, as, dig, house, name, ran, too, back, door, how, new, saw, took, ball, down, if, next, school, tree, be, first, jump, night, seen, two, because, from, just, not, should, us, bed, girl, last, now, sister, very, been, good, laugh, off, so, want, boy, got, little, old, some, water, brother, had, live(d), once, take, way, but, half, love, one, than, were, by, has, made, or, what, call(ed), have, make, out, their, when, came, help, man, out, them, where

Plus
days of the week, months of the year, numbers to twenty, common color words, pupils' names and addresses, name and address of school

Considerable thought has clearly gone into choosing these words. One obvious characteristic is that they nearly all have a single syllable. Doubtless this is based on the belief that short words are easier for the child to handle, which may be true in the early months of language learning when the amount of speech children can absorb is severely limited by their developing memory, but by the age of five it is hardly an important factor in their language use. Indeed, glancing at the early words used up to the age of eighteen months on page 192, a third are longer than one syllable, including two-syllable words, like *daddy, bottle, balloon,* etc. and a few three-syllable words, *banana* and *peekaboo*. There seems little point in choosing words for reading based only on their shortness.

A second criterion used by the National Curriculum seems to be the frequency with which words occur. Virtually all the words on the list are within the 200 or so most frequently used words in English. This has the side effect of making far more of them structure words like *of* and *the* than content words like *house* and *play*, since most of the top words in English are structure words. About half of the forty-five words for the first year are structure words. Structure words are indeed vital to reading English, as they make up a large proportion of any sentence. The National Curriculum has nevertheless left out seventeen other structure words from the first-year list that are in the top fifty words, such as *be* and *had*, and postponed *which*, no. 32, for another two years.

Structure words, however, have rather peculiar characteristics so far as reading and writing are concerned. Their spelling tends to be remembered as a whole rather than each letter being turned into sound. We don't usually read the word *the* as a sequence of the three letters but see it as a whole. Recognizing structure words like *to* and *the* is a different process from reading words like *play* and *ball*. Frequent structure words are linked to a memory of the whole word in the mind, just as we recognize logos like the Nike swoosh. Less frequent content words are built up letter by letter through mental rules for relating sounds and letters: *bat* is converted step by step into sounds, the letter "b" becoming the sound "b," the letter "a" becoming the spoken vowel "a," the letter "t" the consonant "t" (though of course English spelling rules are much more complicated than this).

Furthermore structure words like *can, in, to,* etc., don't actually make sense without content nouns, verbs, or adjectives to pad them out into phrases or sentences. If you took the curriculum literally, first-year children are expected to manage with the nouns *dog*, *day*, and *cat*, the verbs *go*, *come*, *like*, *see*, *play*, and *said*, and a single adjective, *big*. Even if the children had mastered all forty-five words, they could only read variations on *Mum/Dad/the cat/a dog is coming/is going/is looking at it/said no/like me*. All in all, while structure words need to figure prominently in early reading, the reasons for choosing them and the methods for teaching them need to be different from those for content words.

A crucial insight about reading is that starting to read is *not* starting to learn language. Five-year-olds already have an extensive vocabulary in English, not the limited vocabulary of one-year-olds. They can understand and produce a great many words; they simply don't know how to *read* them. Simplifying vocabulary to the most frequent words may be necessary for beginners in a language but hardly for the fluent five-year-old, who is far from a beginner. The *Breakthrough to Literacy* approach to reading started from what children wanted to talk about; if they are interested in hippopotamuses, then *hippopotamus* should be the word they learn to read. The important thing is getting the child to see that reading and writing are communicating things, like speech. The words have to relate to interesting things to read about, not to sterile reading-book sentences such as *Look, Spot*, and *See Jane run*.

Children's writers show us how words that are meaningful to children could be selected. Here are some of the verbs and nouns used in *The Jolly Postman* by Janet and Allan Ahlberg:

Nouns: bicycle, hill, bear, letter, baby, postman, tea, uniform, gingerbread, cottage, witch, bell, bottle, milk
Verbs: read, drink, happen, went, leave, tell, hear, stop, cackle, ride, sing, wobble, feel, pour, begin, put, play

Children can deal with these words when they are read to them; why should they be cut off from everything interesting when they have to read themselves? Lists like those provided by the National Curriculum are only a starting point when thinking about how children can be taught to read and write.

86. How Do You Learn New Vocabulary?

How do you learn the words of a new language? Try learning the following words in Italian. Take as long as you like and then see how well you score on the test on page 289.

1. *forbici*   2. *telefono*   3. *mano*   4. *aereo*   5. *uomo*

6. *bicicletta*   7. *televisione*   8. *chiave*   9. *matita*   10. *barca*

Strategies for acquiring words
The point of this test was not so much to see whether you could learn ten words of Italian as to see how you went about learning them – your learning strategies.

- Did you repeat the words over and over in your mind or aloud? Some people memorize lists of new words or test themselves over and over on packs of word cards, eliminating the ones they know until none are left. This method relies on sheer practice and repetition.
- Did you try to group the words together in common patterns? Some people use "word maps" to link them together, some think about aspects of the word form, say, word endings such as -er or prefixes such as con-. This method relies on organising the words in the mind into logical groups and connections.
- Did you visualize the words or connect them to an incongruous image? One course tried to teach the French *hérisson* (hedgehog) through an image of the English sound-alike "hairy son." This method links words to things you already know.
- Did you try to remember the words as names for pictures? Some

people have a strong visual sense and remember words best through images; others prefer sounds.

- Did you try to pair each word with its translation, *chiave* with *key* etc.? This ties the new language in strongly with the first language, not usually a habit encouraged by teachers. But translation is a traditional way of learning new vocabulary; students still test themselves on word lists in spare moments.
- Did you try to work out the parallels with English words, *telefono* to *telephone, aereo* to *airplane* and so on? This works reasonably when the two languages are related but is less successful when the languages have few things in common, say English and Chinese, unless the word has been borrowed.

All these methods have been used for learning and teaching foreign-language vocabulary. Which works best depends on the individual; no single method is best for everyone.

87. Jazzin' around

JAZZ SLANG

From the 1920s to the 1950s, American jazz musicians spoke a variety of English of their own. This came partly out of the black communities of the South and the urban North, partly out of special terms needed for their music, partly from inventive singers like Cab Calloway of "Minnie the Moocher" fame (*mooch*, "a slow dance"). Often it is not clear whether the words come uniquely from the American jazz world or whether jazz musicians were the first to be noticed using them. Many words, like *cool* and *gig*, have become universal. One notable usage is the meaning reversal in which a word that usually means something bad is used to mean something good, familiar from Michael Jackson's "I'm Bad" and Miles Davis's *Miles Live Evil*. The following list gives examples of some words commonly used in jazz slang with reversed meaning:

bad	insane	terrible
crazy	mean	tough
dirty	a mess	weird
evil	a monster	wild
hard	nasty	

   Some of the musical terms in jazz slang were:
bop: a style originating from Charlie Parker and Dizzy Gillespie in the early 1940s. The term arises from such phrases as *oo-bop-she-bam, oo-ya koo, oo-pa-pa-da, bebop*, and *hay bar re-bop*, i.e. the use of nonsense rhythmic syllables.
gig: a one-night engagement for a group
riff: a short phrase repeated indefinitely, typical of swing-era music
swing: a certain kind of rhythmic feeling. As Fats Waller said when asked what rhythm was, "If you don't know what it is, you ain't

got it." *Swing* also refers to big bands playing a popular 1930s style of jazz, such as those led by Harry James and Artie Shaw.

Drugs played a large part in the lives of jazz musicians of this period, hence the proliferation of drug terms, some of which have spread round the globe.

blow "smoke marijuana"	joint	shit
grass	junk	stuff
H (herion)	mary jane	tea
hash	muggles	viper
hemp	o.z. (ounce of marijuana)	
horse	reefer	

This led to song titles such as "Muggles" and "Viper Mad," though presumably "Tea for Two" was innocuous.

Jazz musicians were also given to nicknames, some of which are genuine, some doubtless made up by jazz fans:

Bird: Charlie Parker, alto sax (several dubious explanations, one to do with his fondness for fried chicken, another to do with his standing in a yard to listen to musicians in a club, hence *Yardbird*, another that it changed from *Charlie > Charl > Yarl> Yard > Yardbird > Bird*)

Hawk: Coleman Hawkins, tenor sax, also known as *Bean*

Lady Day: Billie Holiday, singer, rechristened by Lester Young

Prez: Lester Young, the President, as he was the president of the tenor sax, rechristened by Billie Holiday

Satch/Satchmo: Louis Armstrong, trumpet, abbreviated from *Satchelmouth*, also known as *Pops*

Trane: John Coltrane, tenor and soprano sax

Then there were the musicians with self-conferred titles: *Duke Jordan, Duke Ellington, Count Basie, King Oliver, Sir Charles Thompson,* and *Earl Fatha Hines;* Billie Holiday's mother was known as *the Duchess*. However, *Sir Roland Hanna* apparently had a genuine knighthood awarded by Liberia.

Many dances and dance crazes originated from this early jazz, and some of them are still around. Several names refer to animals believed to move in particular ways.

Black Bottom	Jive	Shag
Bunny hug	Lindy Hop	Shake
Cakewalk	(allegedly because it looked like Lindbergh's plane hopping to get off the ground to fly the Atlantic)	Shimmy
Camel walk		Slow drag
Charleston		Stomp
Cootie crawl		Susie Q
Grind	Mooch	Toddle
Grizzly bear	Sand	Turkey trot
Jitterbug	Scraunch	Walkin' the dog

Other words that may have originated from jazz slang, at least in these senses, are:

big apple, "New York"
bread, "money"
broad, "woman"
cat, "person"
chick, "young woman"
cool, "in fashion/good"
dig, "to like"
face, "person"
far out, "extraordinary"

hip/hipster, "fashionable person"
ofay, "white man"
professor, "pianist in a brothel,"
    e.g. *Professor Longhair*
square, 'unfashionable'
threads, "clothes"
uncool, "not in fashion"
unhip, "not in fashion"

Now that jazz is largely played in festivals, concert halls, and specialist jazz clubs, it no longer seems to go in for this cliquish vocabulary. In an interview on a CD sleeve, Brad Mehldau, a contemporary American pianist, manages to refer to *The Cloud of Unknowing* (a fourteenth-century religious text), Thomas Mann, and Bertolt Brecht.

88. Seven Sieves for Learning a Language

THE EUROCOM APPROACH

A new approach to learning to read another language has been pioneered by the EuroCom Research Center. This grafts the vocabulary of a new language onto the language you already know, your native language, by systematically linking the words to the ones you already know. At the moment EuroCom is only available for European languages, in particular for people switching within the family of Romance languages such as Spanish and French.

The language you already know is the key to the new language you are learning. Many words are known to you once you have been given some tips how to recognise their similarity with your own language. Learning this way involves putting the target language words through seven "sieves." Imagine, then, that you are a speaker of Italian wanting to learn French:

1. *International vocabulary.* First you are told words that are common across languages, in, for instance, articles on international politics: *fiscale, dollari, presidente,* to take a sample from the first page of Italian Google news.
2. *Romance.* Next you concentrate on words that are common to the whole language family – about 500 Latin words are still shared across the Romance languages.
3. *Sound correspondences.* You are told the rules that transform the pronunciation of one language into that of the other: Italian *notte* into French *nuit.* Once you know these rules, you have the key to many French words.
4. *Spelling and pronunciation.* The conventions for linking sounds and letters in French and Italian are explained, again revealing how familiar words are once you have decoded the spelling.

5. *Romance structures.* All Romance languages have nine basic sentence patterns, according to EuroCom. All you need to learn are the differences between Italian and French.
6. *Grammatical endings.* The grammatical endings of words in Romance languages derive from Latin. Knowing how Italian relates to French is enough to unlock many more words.
7. *Compounds.* A clue to many words in another Romance language is the prefixes, roots, and suffixes that make them up, again derived from the same Latin source and recognizable once you can decode them.

And now you're away, not just to another Romance language but to any of the eight included in EuroCom. At least that's the claim.

89. The Visions of Passionate People
SLOGANS OF THE 2000S

Advertisers and politicians latch on to fashionable words to sell their products – remember *vision*, *excellence*, and *mission statement*? The 2000s have seen a plague of the word *passionate*, particularly in the North of England. According to the *Oxford English Dictionary* (*OED*), its main senses are "marked by anger, easily moved, dominated by intense emotion, vehement, moved by deep sexual love." All of these are fairly negative in tone. Being passionate means feeling a strong, uncontrollable emotion.

A quotation from John Donne is typical:

Art is the most passionate orgy within man's grasp.

Or W. B. Yeats:

The best lack all conviction, while the worst
Are full of passionate intensity.

So in what sense should we take remarks such as:

I'm absolutely passionate about the Middle East.

The speaker is angry about it? He's vehement? He's one of Yeats's worst?

How about a hospital that is:

Passionate about patients

Do they love them sexually? Are they extremely angry with them?

The Web soon locates further examples:

Passionate about: concrete ... plants ... travel ... punctuation ... pedaling ... pashmina ... sustainability ... cannabis ... the au pair ... London ... penstemon ... purple ... soft condensed matter ...

Just what strong uncontrollable feelings do people have for these diverse objects?

Of course none of these uses are close to the traditional dictionary meanings. They mean something like "people who care about something." The adjective *passionate* has been back-formed anew from the noun *passion*, stripped of a thousand years of negative meanings. The writers seem unaware of any negative possibilities, otherwise they would hardly confess to being passionate about the au pair. This does English more of a disservice than any of the usual sins decried by newspaper letter-writers and media presenters, such as abuse of the apostrophe or the splitting of infinitives – the deliberate use of a word that sounds vaguely positive with all specific meaning drained from it.

90. Guessing Words in Context

One way of learning new words is to guess what they mean from the contexts in which they occur. We learn the vast majority of words in this accidental way. Nobody explains or defines the twelve words a day we are learning in childhood, except sometimes when we are learning a second language.

How good are you at guessing new words from their context? The test below measures your ability to work out the meanings of words that are new to you. If you know a word already, skip it and go on to the next. Answers are on page 289.

1. Imported zebra mussels clog Northeastern waterways, the Korean **hantavirus** invades Baltimore, and Asian mudfish waddle down Florida's roads.
   hantavirus means something like: ....

2. It was peels at 8-to-8 in the tenth head as the skip stepped up to the **crampit** to deliver his iron.
   crampit means something like: ....

3. The project is to examine structural and functional changes in the organization and stability of fibrillin **microfibrils** in skin.
   microfibrils means something like: ....

4. There was no evidence of valve failure or tissue growth within the valve **annulus**.
   annulus means something like: ....

5. The exact shape of her body was difficult to determine because of her roomy **salwar kamiz**.
   salwar kamiz means something like: ....

6. Sages ... Come from the holy fire, perne in a **gyre**, and be the singing masters of my soul.
   gyre means something like: ....

7. The more **illiquidity** that the financial system can sustain, the greater the level of investment.
   illiquidity means something like: ....

8. The year started with the unexpected collapse of a **wichert** cottage in Harwell.
   wichert means something like: ....

9. But his **coup de maître** came when he evoked the name of revered symbols to describe China's "unshakeable" relationship with Japan.
   coup de maître means something like: ....

10. Women working in manufacturing in the east Midlands told me of their heart-ache at "**shift parenting**."
    shift parenting means something like: ....

11. Activists have campaigned for debt deals to be **disaggregated** from new aid money.
    disaggregated means something like: ....

12. **Stepovers** are often planted at the front of a border to form an attractive low edging.
    stepovers means something like: ....

13. The player blows through the reed to make sound come from the **rackett**. The tone is warm, rich, and versatile.
    rackett means something like: ....

14. The idea of **Sehnsucht** continues to have power today, because what lies at its heart ... is so deeply woven into the fabric of the human condition.
    Sehnsucht means something like: ....

D. Clarke and Paul Nation, two researchers in teaching vocabulary, recommend four stages in guessing the meaning of an unknown word. Their example is the word *crippled* in *Typhoon Vera killed or injured 218 people and crippled the seaport city of Keelung*. To guess its meaning you need to:

i) work out which part of speech the word belongs to: *crippled* must be a verb here because it ends in *-ed* and it occurs between a subject, *Typhoon Vera*, and an object, *the seaport city of Keelung*.

ii) look at the immediate context: typhoons usually do nasty things rather than nice things to places, as we see from the other verbs, *killed* and *injured*. Working out that *crippled* has a negative meaning may be all you need to get the gist of the sentence.

iii) look at the wider context, taking into account the general ways in which information is presented in English, such as cause and effect. *The car crashed; the driver died* is different from *The driver died; the car crashed*. *Typhoon* is clearly a cause, *crippled* an effect, presumably a nasty one to fit the meanings of *killed* and *injured*.

iv) guess the meaning and check whether your guess works: for instance, whether your guess fits the part of speech of *crippled*, whether it contains any prefixes like *re-* or *un-* that convey meaning, and whether it makes sense in the whole sentence.

91. Basic English

In the 1920s the British academics C.K. Ogden and I. A. Richards proposed Basic English, a specially constructed form of English to be used as a "supranational language." Richards was reacting to what he saw as "the world's need for a common language." In a sense this was following the same route as the inventors of artificial languages, such as Esperanto and Volapuk, who wanted to create a vehicle for international communication independent of the control of any nation.

The strength of Basic English over invented languages like Esperanto was that it was based on an existing language and could be created by paring the existing vocabulary and grammar to the minimum. As it didn't have to be created from scratch, unlike Esperanto, it exploited the known strengths of English rather than the unknown features of a new language. Richards saw "a priority for English as the world's 'second' language in the interests of everyone," a goal shared by generations of English teachers.

According to Richards, "Basic English is English made simple by limiting the number of its words to 850, and by cutting down the rules for using them to the smallest number necessary for the clear statement of ideas." All that you need to learn Basic English can be written down on a single sheet of paper. Compare this to standard English, which needs weighty volumes to begin to capture its complexity.

The 850 Words of Basic

Operations (meaning "acts or *operations* of our bodies and of bodies generally") (100 words): *of, when, not, send, north, again, do, I* ... with eighteen verbs, *come, get, give, send* ...

General Things (400): *blood, grass, cough, look, verse, butter, kick, death, level, knowledge* ... all nouns

Picturable Things (200): *potato, stomach, cheese, house, berry, eye,* *school, knife, coat ...*

General Qualities (100): *male, good, fertile, electric, dependent, red, strong, clean, true, violent ...*

Qualities "before the names of things to give some special idea about the thing" (50): *bad, dirty, female, simple, feeble, low, foolish, soft, false ...*

These are to be supplemented by some specialist and international words.

Summary of the Rules of Basic English

* plurals should all end in *s, eyes, schools,* not *children, men,* i.e. all plurals are regular
* other words can be created by using *-er, -ing,* and *-ed* from 300 nouns, *stronger, coughing*
* adverbs can be made from qualifiers by adding *-ly,* (*badly, falsely*), comparatives by adding *more* and *most,* i.e. *more pretty* rather than *prettier*
* questions are made by inverting the word order and adding *do, Do you see him?*
* pronouns, etc. have their full forms: *he/him/his,* rather than *'im,* i.e. don't have the variation in stress and form of ordinary English

And that's essentially it. Everything else you might want to say can be built out of these words and rules. The single-page specifications for Basic English are less complicated than the instructions for operating a digital radio. Its simplicity is only apparent, of course, because it surreptitiously relies on large amounts of English grammar. For instance, English has the word order Subject Verb Object: *The cat chased a mouse,* not Subject Object Verb: *The cat a mouse chased,* as is common in German, or Verb Subject Object: *Chased the cat a mouse,* like Arabic. If you know English, you don't need to learn much to be able to use Basic English; speakers of other languages have a greater burden because of the differences between their first language and the concealed English grammar under the surface of Basic English.

Here are some examples of what Basic English looks like, translated by I. A. Richards himself:

English	Basic English translation
Daniel Defoe, Robinson Crusoe	
It happened one time that going a fishing with him on a calm morning, a fog rose so thick, that though we were not half a league from the shore, we lost sight of it; and rowing, we knew not whither, or which way, we laboured all day and all the next night …	It came about one time that when we had gone fishing on a quiet morning, such a thick mist came up that, though we were not a mile and a half from the land, we were unable to see it. Without any knowledge of where, or even which way we were going, we went on in the boat all that day and all the night after …
The Atlantic Charter	
… Third they respect the right of all peoples to choose the form of government under which they will live; and they wish to see sovereign rights and self-government restored to those who have been forcibly deprived of them.	… Third, they take the view that all nations have the right to say what form of government they will have; and it is their desire to see their self-government and rights as independent nations given back to those from whom they have been taken away by force.

Basic English was taken seriously for many years. In a sense its main objective has now been largely supplanted by English itself. Language teachers have been arguing for a type of English to be used among non-native speakers called English as a Lingua Franca

(ELF). The difference is that ELF grows out of the actual needs of its users. It is not designed in advance by experts but continually created by people trying to communicate with each other, so it is inherently flexible compared with Basic English, which was laid down in advance by its two creators.

92. How to Remember Ten New Words

New information can be remembered by hooking it into something you already know. One technique for doing this involves
memorizing a short poem for the numbers from one to ten:

One's a bun
Two's a shoe
Three's a tree
Four's a door
Five's a hive
Six's sticks
Seven's heaven
Eight's a gate
Nine's a line
Ten's a hen

Then you set about remembering ten items by making an
incongruous mental image connecting each item with a number
on the list. If no. 1 is an elephant, you have to invent an image of an
elephant eating a bun or an elephant inside the bun. And so on for
nine other items. Things remembered in this way can be quickly
recovered from memory, even out of sequence. Elaborate schemes
exist for handling more items at a time, particularly useful for card
players.

93. General Semantics

One of the odd byways in the study of words is general semantics, almost a cult from the 1940s to the 1970s. This theory claimed, quite reasonably, that the way we use language affects the way we deal with the world. A linguist and ex-insurance assessor called Benjamin Lee Whorf wrote about his experiences as a fire inspector. The day shift in a factory had an electric fire on the wall worked by a switch on the wall. The night watchman, however, thought the fire was a rack for hanging up his coat, turned on what he assumed was the light switch and the building caught fire.

Whorf saw language as affecting how we interpret the world. What one person called *turning on a light*, the other called *turning on a fire*; the way they had translated the world into language in their minds had influenced what they did.

Another of Whorf's stories concerned a garage mechanic throwing a cigarette into what he had classified as *waste water* and therefore uninflammable. But it was actually largely made up of oil, highly inflammable, and so duly caught fire. Calling it *waste water* led directly to the fire; it was a language mistake. The way that we describe the world to ourselves through language and the word itself, is sometimes the problem.

This kind of insight was systematized by Count Alfred Korzybski, the founder of the Institute of General Semantics, in 1938 into axioms such as "The map is not the territory," meaning that language is not the same as the real world. In Japan people once had to rescue pictures of the emperor from burning schools, as if the pictures were the man himself. The fact that we say something does not make it true of the real world, only of our beliefs about the world. Slogans like *Peace in our time* and *There is no alternative* do not correspond to anything in the real world.

Korzybski also claimed that our thinking relies too much on dividing the world into a matter of *either/or*, *yes/no*, which he called

Aristotelian logic. A claim like *You're either with us or against us*, used to drum up support for anti-terrorism laws, denies any other possibilities, such as challenges to the underlying premise that there is a vast increase in terrorist activities; it is a case of a simple either/or being imposed on a highly complex set of possibilities. Political discussion is dominated by the idea of *either/or, left/right, capitalist/communist*, etc.; everything is seen as black or white. Human beings would fare better, according to general semantics, if they appreciated the world in its true complexity rather than reducing it to pairs of opposites, *good/evil, peace/war*, and the like.

The cult of general semantics gradually lost contact with the science of semantics that studies the meaning of language. A. E. van Vogt wrote science fiction novels using general semantics principles about superheroes who supposedly applied non-Aristotelian (null-A) logic to their problems, such as *The World of Null-A*, with its hero Gilbert Gosseyn (go sane), though the general implications tended to get lost in the wild swings of his plots.

While general semantics itself proved a dead end, it nevertheless reminds us of the crucial links between language and thinking.

94. Piggy in the Middle
ADDING TO THE MIDDLE OF WORDS

One characteristic of English words is that things can be added to them at the beginning or at the end, but never in the middle – technically called an infix (as opposed to a prefix and a suffix). The word *admit* can have a prefix added at the beginning, *readmit*, or a suffix at the end, *admits*, but not in the middle, *adremit* or *adsmit*. This is quite obvious to English speakers, but not to speakers of Inuktitut, who add bits to words cumulatively, ending up with gigantic specimens such as, *qangatasuukkuvimmuuriaqalaaqtunga* meaning "I'll have to go to the airport."

There are a few exceptions in English where infixes are indeed used. The most common are words like *fanfuckingtastic*, where the word *fucking* has been inserted into *fantastic* to intensify the meaning. The words that can be inserted into other words in this way are those which show extra emotion. Hence they are often swearwords used in exclamations.

95. Simplified Vocabularies

POLITICAL CORRECTNESS AND THOUGHT CONTROL

Those who want to control people's language, whether for good reasons or bad, typically pick on the words they use rather than on their pronunciation or their grammar. Political correctness hinges upon *not* saying words that are believed offensive for one reason or another: don't say *handicapped*, say *disabled*. Political control of language, like Orwell's *Newspeak* (see page 238), is an extreme form of language control, which restricts what people think by controlling what they say.

More benign control, such as Richards and Ogden's Basic English (see page 219), simplifies the vocabulary of English for practical, well-intentioned reasons. If everybody in the world used the same words with the same meaning, international communication would be much easier. And reducing the number of meanings attached to each word might help even more. If, say, the word *reader* meant only "person who reads," not a "member of a library" or "machine for reading" or "senior academic," we would use it with greater clarity and consistency – if that is what we are after.

English as Lingua Franca (ELF) has been proposed to act as a tool that anyone anywhere in the world can use to talk to anyone else, not to be confused with the traditional EFL (English as a Foreign Language). In ELF the simplifications arise from how people talk to each other, for instance being over-explicit, *black color* rather than just *black*, or saving on the sounds, so that the "th"s in *theme* and in *them* are pronounced the same. The strength of ELF is that it is detached from any particular country – you are not linking yourself with, say, the United Kingdom or Canada if you use a neutral form that suits the needs of its users rather than those of native speakers of "standard" English. Nevertheless, many still believe in the importance of a standard language or culture:

for them, learning English implies conforming to a national standard, whether English, Canadian, or Indian, not being a world citizen unattached to any country.

A smaller, more consistent vocabulary could be a boon to second-language users who want to communicate through English despite a poor command of the language. Since 1959, the Voice of America (VOA) has broadcast some of its programs in Special English, which has a vocabulary of 1,500 words listed in an online Word-Book with brief descriptions:

- words for everyday objects
  pig - n. a farm animal used for its meat
- words for world events
  wreckage - n. what remains of something severely damaged or destroyed
- words for science
  substance - n. the material of which something is made (a solid, liquid, or gas)

Wikipedia also has a special section called Simple English Wikipedia, based on the Basic English 850-word list and the VOA Special English Word-Book. Two examples recommended by them are:

Some countries, including Britain and France ... > Some countries, for example Britain and France ...
Carpets are like rugs. > Carpets are similar to rugs.

Like the VOA, Wikipedia does not adopt a systematic approach to grammar, but exhorts writers to keep it simple: for instance, by avoiding the passive:

The bird was eaten by the cat. > The cat ate the bird.

An international language may be required for specific jobs: French was once the language of diplomacy, German that of engineering. Pilots and air traffic controllers use English all over the world. In a nine-hour day at a Turkish airport, the controllers had to deal with 278 pilots, only two of whom were from English-speaking countries. Yet all of them were speaking English. Several crashes have been caused by poor use of English. The Tenerife runway crash in 1977 with 583 dead, still the most in aviation history, is partly attributable to the pilot saying *We are now at take-off*. This could mean either "we are now at the take-off position" – the air traffic controller's interpretation, or "we are now actually taking off" – the pilot's interpretation, possibly based on what it would mean in his native Dutch. The pilot's last words in a fatal crash in China were, in Chinese, *What does "pull up pull up" mean?*

Simplifications of English for flying include changing *Yes* and *No* to the clearer *Affirmative* and *Negative*, changing *Roger* to *Will comply* as *Roger* might mean "I have understood but am taking no action," and changing the names of the Japanese navigation fixes *NOGAL* and *NOGAR*, because Japanese air traffic controllers have trouble distinguishing English "r" and "l." Simplified English is also needed for cabin announcements in emergencies, such as *jump jump* and *brace brace* – the latter hardly within most people's active vocabularies and not directly found in the *Oxford English Dictionary*, an ELF usage as native English requires *yourself – brace yourself*.

Mariners have relied on a simplified English called *Seaspeak*, designed in the 1960s to enable ships to talk to each other. It was created to prevent problems such as those encountered with the stranding of an oil tanker in Milford Haven when a Chinese tug was unable to help because its crew had such minimal knowledge of English that the authorities had to borrow a cook from a Chinese restaurant to act as interpreter. Incidentally, the tanker was owned by Norwegians and crewed by Russians. Ships at sea need some reliable form of communication between such multilingual seamen.

The interesting thing about Seaspeak is not so much its simple vocabulary as its way of showing grammar through "message markers." If you want to make a statement, you start the sentence with the marker *Information*:

Information: I need food.

Then you give your reason:

Reason: I am hungry.

Instead of just asking a question, you start with the marker *Question*:

Question: Why are you hungry?

And the reply starts with *Answer*:

Answer: I haven't eaten for three days.

The intention is to make each sentence unambiguous. There is no problem understanding whether:

Can you lift that chair?

is a request or a question if it is labelled:

Request: Can you lift that chair? (and put it by the fireplace)
Question: Can you lift that chair? (and show me how strong you are)

Seaspeak is now largely superseded as an international standard by *SMCP* (Standard Marine Communication Phrases).

Learners of English form another large group with a need for simple vocabulary. Learners can't take in the whole dictionary in a gulp, so teachers have to decide which words to prioritize, usually choosing to start with words that are highly frequently used, such as *man*, or words whose meanings are easy to get across, like *chair*. My own beginners' coursebook for English, *People and Places*, used a vocabulary of 850 words; most beginners' books have a similar figure.

Some dictionaries for learners of English use a simplified vocabulary for definitions, avoiding such well-known problems as the definition of *cat* as "feline quadruped" – the words for explaining a word should be simpler than the word itself. In addition, for many years publishers have provided simplified readers for students using limited vocabulary. The Longman Bridge Series, for instance, kept to the most frequent 7,000 words and explained all of those outside a 3,000-word limit.

96. Schizophrenic

For a generation, people have been guarded with their words to avoid sexism, racism, and the like – what a newspaper once called "petty bourgeois linguistic anti-racism."

Let us take a less familiar example of words to be avoided. Some people with schizophrenia are upset by the use of *schizophrenic* to mean, as the COBUILD English dictionary puts it, people who "seem to have very different purposes or opinions at different times," i.e. they switch from one personality to another. The *Oxford English Dictionary* talks only of a transferred or figurative use without being more specific.

This use of the word shows a misunderstanding of schizophrenia as an illness. Although schizophrenia has many possible symptoms, hearing voices is more likely to be crucial to the diagnosis than having multiple or variable personalities. The use reinforces a popular interpretation that schizophrenia means having two personalities. Eugen Bleuler originally coined the word *schizophrenia* in 1910 to mean "disruption of mental functions," not "multiple personalities."

People are very careful when they refer to other diseases. No one would be comfortable with *I feel rather spastic/diabetic/tubercular/HIV about this*. So why should *I feel schizophrenic about this* be acceptable? To quote Irving Gottesman, an authority on schizophrenia, "Using the terms schizophrenia or schizophrenic to refer to the foreign policy of the United States, the stock market, or any other disconfirmation of one's expectations does an injustice to the enormity of the public health problems and profound suffering associated with this most puzzling disorder of the human mind."

In the case of *schizophrenia,* despite many finding this usage objectionable, writers use it casually every day of the week. On Google News the day I wrote this about half the examples of *schizophrenic* quite properly referred to the actual disease – *schizophrenic man* or *schizophrenic delusions*. But the rest fell straight into the trap: *the schizophrenic Sox* – the whole team has been diagnosed? *We refuse to be schizophrenic* – if only one could indeed treat the illness by refusing it. *Ninja gaiden is a schizophrenic of a game* – hallucinating and hearing voices?

This meaning of *schizophrenic* is so everyday that it is taken for granted. And of course anybody has the right to make a word mean what they like. But in this case it is more than rude, it is ignorant. Avoiding using *schizophrenic* in the loose sense may not cure the disease, but it may reassure sufferers that at least we are not unaware of the nature of their condition. I suspect I may be the only person to have complained about the "Thought for the Day" segment on the *Today* radio program for using *schizophrenic* in this way. Not that this has had much effect; I recently heard the boss of a firm of headhunters on the *Today* program, who was dealing with a question about divided interests in job descriptions, shrug it off by saying that there was no way of *schizophrenia being a major qualification for a job.* Job-hunters with any history of mental illness needn't bother with his firm, obviously.

One of the themes of this book is how what we say links to what we do. Does saying a thing make it so? Does labelling children *Down's syndrome* rather than *mongoloid* cause them to be treated any better or worse? Or does *not* saying something change anything? If we avoid the word *coloured*, does that stop people being discriminated against? The word *schizophrenic* is one more case in which it is obviously courteous to sufferers not to use it in an inappropriate way, but doing this may have little effect on the treatment of those with mental illnesses. Changing the words doesn't automatically change the world.

97. On First-Name Terms

Meeting someone called Mr. Elvis Presley, you have a choice whether to address him as *Elvis, Mr. Presley* or *Presley*. One factor governing your choice is formality. On formal occasions, when you don't know people very well, title plus family name, *Mrs. Jones*, may be appropriate. First names (such as Grace) are for informal use with friends and relatives. For the older generation, using the first name was a privilege reserved for intimate friends. So older patients in hospitals are offended when the staff attempt to address them as *Betty* rather than *Mrs. Jones*, even if the intention is just to be friendly.

Indeed, this unease at strangers using first names is more widespread than many companies or organisations realize. Why should I believe in the competence of a waiter called *Joe* or a cabin attendant called *Gerald*? They are professionals serving the public, not instant friends on Facebook. A logical reason for names being available is to identify them in case of complaint. Can you imagine complaining about a policewoman called *Jane*, a doctor called *Pete*, or a judge called *Sarah*?

One of the reasons for our sensitivity to first names is that formality is overlain by a second system of social power. First names are used by bosses to subordinates:

BOSS: Good morning, Helen.
SECRETARY: Good morning, Mr. Jones.

But not vice versa. Using the first name shows you have power over someone when they cannot reciprocate first names with you, deriving from the usual parent-to-child use – how common even now is it for children of whatever age to call their parents by their first names? – or teacher to pupil.

Relics of this power are seen in the habit in newspaper headlines of referring to women but not men by their first names: *Venus steers her sister to promised title* and *Laura, 14, becomes the new darling of Wimbledon* but *Finalists Federer, Nadal know each other well* and *Mistakes cost Lewis Hamilton pole.* When I first started teaching, I used to call students by their first names, thinking I was being informal and friendly. However, they always replied with my title and surname, and I realized that they perceived this as a power ploy of unreciprocated first-name use.

98. Using Words in Odd Ways

Any person can use words in a new way – provided other people can make out what they mean. Here are some sentences from diverse sources that are unlikely to have occurred in this form before, yet are perfectly comprehensible:

You'll open wide him—I'll subdivide him. (Guinevere and Knight in the film *Camelot*)

The Hungarian Grand Prix is now on with a vengeance. (commentator)

If you want to make sure you're eating enough of fiber, it's worth knowing that there's as much fiber in twenty-one new potatoes as you find in just a single bowl. (TV commercial)

The 2008 Olympics showed off many peculiar uses of words by sports commentators. A *final qualification* meant someone had qualified to be in the final, not the last degree they had received. An *Olympian* was not a Greek god like Zeus but somebody who competed in the Olympics (first used in 1977, *OED*). *Medaling* meant to gain a medal (*OED*, 1966). Perhaps oddest of all was that the UK team was consistently called *Team GB*, not the *GB team*. Come on – if you speak English, there's a rule that modifiers precede nouns – *red sky* not *sky red*. Presumably the commentators were employed by the Broadcasting Corporation British, Television Independent or Television Sky. If you're going to wax patriotic about national sides, you might at least have pride in the rules of your national language.

99. Warning: Words Can Damage Your Health

NEWSPEAK

If thinking depends upon language, then controlling people's language is a way of controlling their thoughts. This is the logic behind the banning of discriminatory terms such as *Paki* and *chairman*: if you don't know the nasty words, you can't think the nasty thoughts, and thus racism and sexism will be wiped out. No one can object to removing language that deliberately insults people for no just cause.

One example has been the changes in English over thirty years in the use of pronouns. English pronouns are marked for gender: female objects are referred to as *she*, male objects as *he* and sexless objects as *it*. This leaves English people in a quandary when they need to use a singular pronoun without knowing the gender of the person. The solution used to be that the masculine *he* referred to both sexes:

If a passenger needs an extra blanket, he should ask the flight attendant.

But people objected that this implied a precedence of males over females; women seemed to be an afterthought. One alternative was to make it clearer by substituting *he or she*:

If a passenger needs an extra blanket, he or she should ask the flight attendant.

or the unpleasant written form still beloved by students, *s/he*.

An alternative is to break the number barrier by using the neutral *they* in the singular:

If a passenger needs an extra blanket, they should ask the flight attendant.

In the 1970s some authors deliberately used *he* and *she* in alternate chapters, a self-conscious and intrusive way of writing. Nevertheless, studies of English newspapers have shown a decline of generic *he* over the last decades. Between 1960 and the present, the number of *she*s in *Time* magazine almost doubled, while the number of *he*s went down by 14 percent. English is less prone to include women in the male *he* than it was before.

But the process of deliberate change to the language can be used for evil ends. If we ban the word *freedom*, how can we have the concept of being free? The most famous fictional example of language control is *Newspeak* in George Orwell's *1984*. This is specially designed by Big Brother "not only to provide a medium of expression for the world-view and mental habits proper to the devotees of Ingsoc [English Socialism] but to make all other forms of thought impossible."

Newspeak works by simplifying the vocabulary into three groups of words:

A: Words for everyday life
Words for everyday things remain the same except for three factors:

- rather than a word having many possible meanings, say, the range of meanings associated with *table*, like "water table," "to table a motion," etc., a Newspeak word has a single meaning: *table* means "a flat-topped piece of furniture" and nothing else. The A-group vocabulary thus expresses only "simple, purposive thoughts."

- one word can belong to many parts of speech. Why should a word be either a noun or a verb or an adjective when it can be all of them? So *a think* is a noun; *to think* a verb; *thinkful* an adjective; *thinkwise* an adverb.

- why have two words for *good* and *bad* when you can say *good* and *ungood*? *Black* and *white* when you can say *black* and *unblack*? If you want to intensify the meaning, you can say *plusgood* or even *doubleplusungood*. This cuts down the number of words in the language and so, Big Brother hopes, the number of concepts available to its speakers.

B: Words "deliberately constructed for political purposes"

Newspeak aims to provide a limited range of ideas biased in one direction, achieved by making up new compound words, as in *goodthink*, *crimethink* (thought crime) and *think pol* (thought police). These have only a single meaning: *goodsex* means only "married sex for reproduction"; any other sex is *sexcrime*. Words can be forced to have contrary meanings: a *joycamp* is forced labor. The sting can be taken out of words by combining their initial parts: the ministries in Oceania are *Minitrue* (Ministry of Truth, i.e. propaganda), *Minipax* (Ministry of Peace, i.e. war) and *Miniluv* (Ministry of Love, i.e. law and order). The simplified vocabulary systematically distorts the world by forcing its users into a single channel of thinking.

C: Scientific and technical terms

Obviously, technical jobs do need additional vocabulary, such as *spanner* and *voltage*. But these are restricted to a particular technical skill rather than having more widespread use – there is no word for "science" in Newspeak. And, like lists A and B, the words have only a single meaning apiece.

Put together, these amount to thought control via language so that "the expression of unorthodox opinions, above a very low level, was well-nigh impossible."

In some ways George Orwell was mirroring the views of his time about how language affects thinking. His simplification of English into Newspeak is clearly based on the Basic English put forward by Ogden and Richards (see page 219). His idea of language affecting thinking is related to the ideas of General Semantics suggested by Count Korzybski (see page 224) and to linguistic relativity (see page 108). But Richards created Basic English as an aid to communication; Korzybski thought better language led to better thinking. They regarded language as a tool to improve people's lives. It is Orwell who saw the dark side of a government controlling its people through language. If they never hear alternative views, they don't know that they exist – essentially Chomsky's view of the American media.

Several science fiction novels have explored how people can be controlled through language. In *The Languages of Pao*, Jack Vance creates a world where each language allows only certain ways of thinking: Valiant is the language for solders, Technicant for technicians, and Cogitant for scientists. In *Babel-17*, Samuel R. Delany imagines an intergalactic terrorist controlled by a perfectly logical language.

Is Newspeak just fiction? George Orwell had an amazing feel for English and was reporting tendencies that were already present in the language. For example, he poured scorn on the fashion for *not un-* rather than positive statements – *A not unblack dog was chasing a not unsmall rabbit across a not ungreen field* – a habit still not uncommon among a not inconsiderable number of not unimportant people.

Much of our everyday life is expressed through words that might well have been created in Newspeak. *Friendly fire* is modeled on *joycamp*; *political correctness* is *thoughtcrime*, except that it hasn't made it to *polcor* yet. *The peace process* is a vague metaphor that forces us into a way of thinking, getting us used to the idea that peace is never achievable and we are always at war. It gets even obscurer in the extended versions from media presenters, *this sends an arrow into the heart of the peace process* or *bolstering the faltering peace process*.

Other expressions seem to show a similar disconnection between words and reality; what could Sebastian Coe mean when he said the upcoming 2012 Olympics *kicked off a catalyst for regeneration*? *Excellence* no longer means "the best" but "the standard," as in *NICE* (the National Institute for Health and Clinical Excellence). Looking at countries referred to as democratic around the word, *democracy* now means little more than "people I approve of." Even if the media are not deliberately implementing Newspeak control over our thoughts, it certainly feels like it.

100. How Do You Say "No"?
NEGATION ACROSS LANGUAGES

In English there are two main types of question: open questions, that start with a question word like *how* or *who* and require a full answer:

> *How do you take your coffee?*
> *Black with two sugars/Milk with no sugar …*

and yes/no "inversion" questions, which start with an auxiliary like *do* or *can* and require an answer with *yes* or *no*:

> *Do you like guavas?*
> *Yes, I do/No, I don't.*

Answering a yes/no question seems quite straightforward: the core of the answer is *yes* or *no* according to whether you agree or disagree with the other person. So translating *yes* and *no* into other languages should be no problem. The meanings of *yes* and *no* must be true everywhere, regardless of what the actual words for them may be.

However, language is never as simple as that. In English, positive or negative questions (ones with *not*, etc.) can both have the answer *Yes* or *No*.

Are you married?	*Yes, I am.*	The question is positive; the listener agrees	*Yes*
Are you married?	*No, I'm not.*	The question is positive; the listener disagrees	*No*
Aren't you married?	*Yes, I am.*	The question is negative; the listener agrees	*Yes*
Aren't you married?	*No, I'm not.*	The question is negative; the listener disagrees	*No*

Other languages handle these types of questions and answers differently, as the following table, based on the work of John Catford, a British linguist, shows.

	positive/ negative question	listener agrees/disagrees	English	French	Japanese
Did you? I did	+	+	yes	*oui*	*hai*
Didn't you? I did	–	+		*si*	*iie*
Did you? I didn't	+	–	no	*non*	
Didn't you? I didn't	–	–			*hai*

For English it does not matter whether the question is positive or negative. A positive question such as *Is he an actor?* can be answered *Yes* or *No*, as can a negative question, *Isn't he an actor?*

- In French, agreeing with a positive question means answering *oui*, but agreeing with a negative question means answering *si*. French has two ways of agreeing where English has one; it depends whether the question is positive or negative in form.

- In Japanese, agreeing with a positive question and disagreeing with a negative question both involve answering *hai*. Conversely, agreeing with a negative question or disagreeing with a negative question means saying *iie*. In Japanese you stick to the same grammatical form in your answer; you answer with *hai* whether you agree or disagree – extremely hard for an English speaker to grasp.

- In Latin the emphasis shifts to the form of the question. The question word *ne* asks an open question that can be answered with *yes* or *no*. A *num* question, however, implies a *no* answer; *nonne* a *yes* answer.

An English parallel is found in so-called tag questions, a common feature of conversation, some say used more by women than by men.

You like guavas, don't you?
He hates politics, doesn't he?
You will be there, won't you?

How do you answer a tag question? Here an extra piece of information is needed: whether the voice goes up or down on the tag question. The rising or falling intonation pattern forces an answer on the other person:

Television is boring, isn't it?   Falling pitch expects the answer *yes*.
Television isn't boring, is it?   Falling pitch expects the answer *no*.
Television is boring, isn't it?   Rising pitch expects either *yes* or *no*.
Television isn't boring, is it?   Rising pitch expects *yes* or *no*.

This complicated system gives rise to everyday problems for learners of English. If *You're coming tonight, aren't you?* gets the answer *No*, the speaker will be very surprised and won't know what has gone wrong. In particular the English intonation system conflicts with the Chinese tone system, in which words change meaning according to their intonation pattern: for instance, *li zi* (rising tone) means "pear"; *li zi* (fall, rise) means "plum" and *li zi* (falling) means "chestnut."

101. How Many Words Do You Know?

ADVANCED WORDS TEST

This tests the size of your vocabulary by seeing how many of the least frequent words in the language you know – the more frequent ones are tested in the Basic Words Test on page 11. The Advanced Words Test covers the words in the British National Corpus from the most frequent 20,000 band up to 150,000+. The *Oxford English Dictionary* has been checked to make certain they actually exist and to check their meanings.

Complete the definitions. All the spaces are the same size, so they do not provide clues to the number of letters. Give up when it becomes just guessing – few people get near the end. Then check your answers (see page 290) and fill in the profile with the answers.

Band F: Words up to 50,000 in frequency

1. a chemical for killing unwanted insects, etc. is a p.....................
2. the quality of being a single whole is a u.....................
3. to spell something out in detail is to a..................... it
4. a white metallic element is b.....................
5. one kind of Italian-derived sausage is a s.....................
6. a tall drinking vessel with a handle is a t.....................
7. a type of brain chemical is s.....................
8. the account of a recently dead person's life is their
   o.....................
9. a channel in the ground made by water is a g.....................
10. a distinctive group of people in North-East Spain are
    C......................

Band G: Words up to 100,000 in frequency

11. something to do with the skull is c.......................

12. a hooded Indian snake is a c.......................

13. a place where many troops live together is a g.......................

14. interwoven rods and laths make a building material called w.......................

15. a two-masted, strongly built boat is a k.......................

16. a sailor's word for a clumsy fellow is a l.......................

17. the effects of wind, rain, etc. on objects is w.......................

18. a fish that breathes with lungs as well as gills is a l.......................

19. a person of high rank is a g.......................

20. a person who speaks only one language is a m.......................

Band H: Words up to 150,000 in frequency

21. a small kind of French cake is a m.......................

22. a person who shaves off small pieces of wood is a w.......................

23. the three wise men from the East were the M.......................

24. something to do with the skin is d.......................

25. the main force of an attack is the b.......................

26. a sandy hollow on a golf course is a b.......................

27. a tropical disease, seldom fatal, is d.......................

28. a member of a Hungarian military force is a h.......................

29. in Roman days, a person acting as governor of a province was a p.......................

30. in days of old, a person who kept an inn was a t.......................

Band I: Words beyond 150,000 in frequency

31. a person who reports proceedings of a group to another group is a r.......................

32. a million-millionth of a second is a p.......................

33. a severe setback in the economy is a r.......................

34. a baby that still lives primarily on milk is u.......................

35. a person who is legally able to vote is e.......................

36. a heavy wheel used to store power is a f.......................

37. an inscription engraved on stone is l.......................

38. when a car shakes violently it j.......................

39. a small kind of bat is a p.......................

40. an African freshwater fish often found in aquariums is a t.......................

102. The Longest Word

In a sense there is no longest word in English: any word can be made longer by adding something. The longest word when I was a schoolboy was allegedly *antidisestablishmentarianism*. But you can add a *quasi-* and an *-ish*: *quasi-antidisestablishmentarianismish*. Almost any word can be made longer with prefixes and suffixes. Similarly, there is no longest sentence, as any sentence can be made longer: *It's hot, it's very hot, it's very very hot.*

It is apparently easy to devise lengthy names for chemical compounds: the *Oxford English Dictionary* for example, claims *pneumonoultramicroscopicsilicovolcanoconiosis* (forty-five letters) as the longest. If we take hyphens into account, the longest word in the British National Corpus, according to the linguist Geoffrey Leech and colleagues, is *oral-aggressive-anal-retentive-come-and-see-me-five-times-a-week-for-years-at-vast-expense-or-how-do-I-know-you're-really-committed.*

Other languages go in for more adventurous compounding, as in the classic German example, *Donaudampfschiffahrtsgesellschaft* ("Danube steamship travel company"). But the prize goes to languages like Inuktitut that pack meanings together without dividing them into words: *Illujuaraalummuulaursimannginamalittauq* ("But also, because I never went to the really big house").

103. Words for Mother and Father

In many languages, words for "mother" tend to start with an "m": *ma, mère, Mutter* ..., words for "father" with a "p/f/v/t": *pa, père, Vater* ... The anthropologist George Murdock analyzed words for relatives in 474 languages, coming up with the following:

Languages in which words for "mother" start with "ma/me/no/ne"

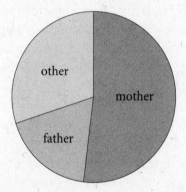

Over half the words (52 percent) for relatives starting with "ma/me/no/ne" meant "mother."

Languages in which words for "father" start with "pa/po/ta/to"

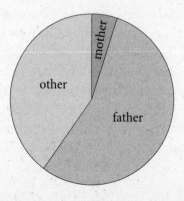

Over half the words (55 percent) for relatives starting with "pa/po/ta/to" meant "father." Wherever you come from in the world, it is good odds that your word for "mother" starts with an "m" or an "n" and your word for "father" with a "p" or a "t."

Murdock presents it as an interesting fact, and no one has ever really disputed it. But what could the reason be? Suppose you put yourself in the position of a baby. You're looking at someone's face as they speak to you. The only sounds you can "see" them make are with the lips and the tongue near the front of the mouth; the rest are produced invisibly inside the mouth or throat. Hence babies are likely to first of all learn sounds in which the lips move or close, like "p," "b" and "m," because they can see how they are produced. They control their own lips to imitate the adults' (itself no mean feat – how do they know their lips correspond to the adult's?) and so are likely to start producing lip sounds rather than ones that are produced invisibly.

An alternative explanation is that the easiest way for babies to make a consonant is to open and close the lips, getting a "p" or "b" sound, or to keep the lips closed and divert the air to the nose to get an "m." The simplest way of making a vowel is to have the mouth open and the tongue at the back of the mouth, yielding "u" and "a" sounds. So babies' first sounds are going to be *ma*, leading to "m" mother words such as *mom* and *ma*; using the lips leads to "p" father words, whether *pa*, *Vater* or *père*.

Yet another possibility is that the first controlled sounds that babies produce are often a stream of *bababa* or *mamama* syllables, called babbling – *mama* has been heard from babies two weeks old. Parents in all countries listen to the *ma*s and *pa*s produced by their babies and fondly imagine they are hearing their names. The words for mother and father come from the first consonants that human babies can produce, to which parents have universally assigned the meaning they want to hear – "mother" and "father." Yet while this theory explains the things common to mother/father words, it does not account for the clear-cut difference between "p" father words and "m" mother words in so many languages.

104. From Pillar to Post

OPPOSITES

Everybody is familiar with the idea of opposites – pairs of words with opposite meaning – *black* and *white* or *plus* and *minus*. But things can be opposites in many different ways. Here is a selection of some of the types of opposites that have been described by D. Cruse. While the differences seem clear-cut intuitively, they are hard to pin down in words.

Complementaries
The meaning of one word complements the meaning of the other.
- **interactive verbs:** the action of one verb leads to a response which the other verb denies: you can't have both.
  Members of the armed forces are sworn … to *obey* all lawful orders and have an affirmative duty to *disobey* all unlawful orders.
  You *accept* an offer or you *refuse* it.
  You *yield* to temptation or you *resist* it.
- **satisfactive verbs:** if the action of one verb is successful, the other is not.
  If at first you don't *succeed*, *try*, *try* again.
  If you *aim* at nothing, you will *hit* it.
  Those who *seek* will *find*.
- **counteractive verbs:** one action is aggressive, the other makes a defense against it.
  He *defended* his title successfully without *submitting*.
  One brother *succeeded* in business, the other *failed*.

Antonyms
These consist of polar opposites which can't coexist; they are usually asymmetrical pairs, with one word having a negative marker such as *dis-* or *un-*.

like/dislike, increase/decrease, accelerate/decelerate

Sometimes one of the pair has vanished, at least for this meaning, as in *unkempt*, *disarming*, and *insomnia*, which do not have the opposites *kempt*, *arming*, and *somnia*.

Directional opposites
Antipodals: general directions with extreme limits – you can't go further in either direction.

    from top to bottom, cellar/attic, full/empty, peak/foot, front/back

    running from pillar to post

Counterparts: reverse irregularities in a surface

    convex/concave, ridge/groove, bump/dent, hill/valley

    stalactites/stalagmites – "When the mites go up, the tights come down"

Reversives: movements in opposite directions

    enter/leave, lengthen/shorten, tie/untie

    rise/fall – "the greater the rise the harder the fall"

Converses: the direction of one thing relative to another

    above/below, before/after, ancestor/descendant, doctor/patient

So English has a range of subtle concepts of what it means to be opposite. Our vocabulary is not just large numbers of separate words; they are linked together in a network of meanings, partly through opposites. The individual words are only a starting point. Getting a fuller picture of how people process words or how children acquire them means looking at the networks in the mind linking *full* and *empty*, *before* and *after*, and all the others.

105. Breeze of the Death

FILM TITLES IN TRANSLATION

Films are often shown under different names in different countries rather than having straight translations. Do the back-translated rewordings actually seem the same as what we would call the "real" title?

James Bond films – titles in other languages

Dr No
> 007 is the Killing Number (Japan)
> Agent 007: Mission: Kill Dr. No (Denmark)

Goldfinger
> Fingers of Gold (Argentina)

From Russia with Love
> 007 is Being Chased (Denmark)
> Agent 007 Sees Red (Sweden)
> Hearty Kisses from Russia (Quebec)
> Love Greetings from Moscow (Germany)

Diamonds are Forever
> 007 Averted the Diamond Gang (China)
> A Cascade of Diamonds (Italy)
> Diamond Fever (Germany)

Live and Let Die
> They're the Ones Who Will Die (Japan)

The Man with the Golden Gun
> The Man with the Golden Colt (Germany)

For Your Eyes Only
> Agent 007: Strict Confidence (Denmark)
> From a Deadly Viewpoint (Sweden)

A View to a Kill
> Moving Target (Italy)
> The Beautiful Prey (Japan)

Dangerously Yours (France)
In the Face of Death (Germany)
The Living Daylights
007: High Tension (Spain)
Icecold Mission (Sweden)
Breeze of the Death (Germany)
Death is Not a Game (France)
Die Another Day
Death Can Wait (Italy)

Studio Ghibli Films

Going from Japanese to another language has similar effects.
Hauro no ugoku shiro
Howl's Moving Castle
The Incredible Wandering Castle
Neko no ongaeshi
The Cat Returns
Sen to Chihiro no kamikakushi
Spirited Away
Chihiro's Journey
Tonari no Totoro
My Neighbour Totoro
Hotaru no haka
Tombstone for Fireflies
Grave of the Fireflies
Heisei tanuki gassen pompoko
Pompoko
The Raccoon War
Majo no takkyubin
Kiki's Delivery Service
The Witch's Express Mail

106. Does a *Méiguì* Smell as Sweet as a Rose?

"A rose by any other name would smell as sweet." Is it true? Suppose we make up a new word, *splont*. This could mean anything at all, from a new kind of garden plant –*There's a fine display of splonts in my garden* – to a way of jumping – *He splonted over the ravine* – or a new infectious disease – *I'm afraid you've got a bad case of the splonts*. The word *splont* doesn't mean anything until its meaning is fixed by someone saying it in a sentence.

The link between the word and its meaning is arbitrary, as Juliet was well aware. At some point English people agreed to call one flower a *rose*, and another a *geranium*, but they could have agreed to call them exactly the opposite. The philosopher Ludwig Wittgenstein said that "a word has the meaning someone has given to it." In principle we all accept that there is no necessary connection between the letters and sounds of a word and its meaning: a *rose* could equally well be called a *geranium* or a *splont*.

Otherwise it would be hard to explain why different languages have different words. We would all have the same vocabulary whether we spoke Chinese, Maltese, Greek or any other language. A rose would not be called a *méiguì* in Chinese, a *warda* in Maltese, or a *triantafyllo* in Greek.

Some words in different languages are obviously similar because they are historically related. A rose is *rose* in French and *rosa* in Spanish because they all go back to the Latin *rosa*. Or a language may just borrow the word, as happened with Japanese *rozu* and Basque *arrosa*. But these similarities are to do with the history of words, not with any intrinsic link between the word *rose* and a particular flower.

However much it is intellectually possible to accept that the links between words and meanings are arbitrary, it is impossible to get rid of the feeling that there is more to it than that. In our everyday lives, the names of objects do somehow reflect their meaning. Why else would parents agonize over choosing names for their children? Is there any basis for this gut feeling that words do really connect with particular things?

A few groups of letters and sounds in English do seem to possess a meaning, as discussed on page 126. Words starting with *squ-*, for example, seem to be negative in meaning, like *squalid* and *squalor*. The COBUILD dictionary based on actual English usage has twenty-four words starting with *squ-*. By my count, twelve of them have a negative meaning, such as *squeal* and *squalor*, and none have a positive meaning. The only ones that have a neutral meaning are *square*, *squid*, and *squad*, and even then you might take it amiss if someone called you *square*, *squid-like*, or a *squaddie*.

Furthermore, many *squ-* words have to do with liquid, *squelch*, or impact, *squash*. Statistically it is hard to prove a connection; any small sample of words starting with a particular sound is bound to share some feature by accident. But such links are self-reinforcing; once we have picked up the negative vibe about *squ-*, we are not going to use it for desirable things: a new instant coffee is unlikely to be called *Squoffy* or a perfume *Eau de squisho*. Even if the meaning of words is arbitrary in a logical sense, human beings try all the time to make sense of words.

An amazing link between words and meanings is found in the names that Ashantis give their children. A child born on a Monday is called *Monday* in Ashanti, on Tuesday *Tuesday*, and so on. But people believe that children born on particular days have particular characteristics. Monday's children are quiet and peaceful, Wednesday's are quick-tempered and aggressive, rather like the rhyme:

Monday's child is fair of face
Tuesday's child is full of grace
Wednesday's child is full of woe …

Sure enough, statistics from courts in Kenya show that more violent crimes are committed by people called Wednesday than by those called Monday. Presumably what happens is that being a Wednesday person means everyone expects you to be violent and therefore you've got a reputation to live up to: "Oh, she's a typical Wednesday, we've got to make allowances." The same self-fulfilling prediction is probably true of astrology. People born under a particular sign will find their behavior interpreted in this way and fed back to them: "He's bound to be intellectual, he's a Gemini."

Perhaps the solution is the way that speech sounds are interpreted by the human ear. According to the phonologist John Ohala's Frequency Code, described later on page 268, high-pitched vowels suggest "small" things and therefore go with lack of importance; low-pitched vowels suggest "big" things, and so go with importance.

Children, too, are convinced that there are links between the forms of words and their meanings. At an early age they believe, for example, that big things are referred to with big words – *hippopotamus* and *dinosaur*, small things with small words like *ant* and *mouse*. Bilingual children are faster to see that there is no link between word size and meaning: a *horse* is big but *bacteria* are small.

107. Addresses

In the English-speaking world, addresses start with the narrowest location – the house name or number – and expand to wider and wider areas – progressively street, district, town, county/province/state, country – as seen below for England and Canada. Spain and France follow similar systems, with variations over where the postal code belongs.

In Hong Kong, addresses start with the widest area – Hong Kong – and then get more precise step by step: area, district, street, number. Korea and China have similar systems. Addresses in the Far East locate an individual within the whole society and then gradually zoom in to a close-up. Addresses in other parts of the world define the individual within wider and wider contexts of the society – expand to a long-shot. This is an example of the distinction made by the social psychologist Geert Hofstede between individualist societies, in which individuals count, and collectivist societies that put the emphasis on groups. How we give our address shows our view of the world and our own place within it.

15 Church Lane (number, street)
Stoke Newington (district)
London (town/city)
N16 5EW (postal code)
England (country)

Japan (country)
780-0985 (postal code)
Kochi-ken (prefecture)
Kochi-shi (city or county) Minamikuma (district name)
5-chome (block number, if any)
117-25 (area number plus house number)

350 Prince Arthur W. Apt.# 1021 (number, street, flat number)
  Montreal, QC (district, province)
    Canada H2X 3R4 (country, postal code)

Hong Kong
  Kowloon
    Hung Hom (district)
      Laguna Verde (housing estate)
        Phase 5
          Block 23
            8th Floor
            Flat D

Madam Kwan's Restaurant
  Lot 420/421,
    Level 4,
      Suria KLCC,
        KL City Center (i.e. Kuala Lumpur)

Seoul City (city)
  Kang-nam-gu (district)
    Sinsadong 25 bungi 4 ho (dong or street plus house number)
      Dae-Han-Min-Kook (country)
        123-456 (postal code)

"Restaurant La Souris Verte"
  52, Rue Sainte Anne (number plus street)
    75002 Paris (postal code plus town)

108. Relatives

Everybody in the world has the same number of potential biological relatives; you can't escape from your family. However, languages express family relationships in different ways.

For example, English does not distinguish between your mother's family and your father's family, so your father's father and your mother's father are both your *grandfather*. In Swedish your mother's father is your *morfar*, your father's father your *farfar*, your mother's mother your *mormor*, and your father's mother your *farmor*, laid out in the table below. Thai and Hindi make the same distinctions. Indeed, some dialects of English or individual families do distinguish between their *nana* and their *nan*. And of course if English speakers need to be precise, they can talk about their *maternal grandmother* and their *paternal grandmother*, but this is hardly everyday language.

The same with aunts and uncles: in Swedish there is a different word for your father's sister and your mother's sister, *faster* and *moster*; one word, *aunt*, does for both in English.

Many languages also recognize seniority by age. In Thai, your father's elder sister is your *pa*, your father's younger sister is your *are*. Both are covered by, *aunt*, in English (and we haven't even looked at the mother's brothers and sisters).

	English	Swedish	Thai
Female parent	mother	*mor*	*mae*
Male parent	father	*far*	*phor*
Mother's male parent	grandfather	*morfar*	*dta*
Father's male parent	grandfather	*farfar*	*pu*
Mother's female parent	grandmother	*mormor*	*ya*
Father's female parent	grandmother	*farmor*	*yai*
Father's brother	uncle	*farbror*	
Mother's brother	uncle	*morbror*	

	English	Swedish	Thai
Father's sister	aunt	*faster*	
Mother's sister	aunt	*moster*	
Father's elder brother	—		*lung*
Father's younger brother or sister	—		*are*
Father's elder sister	—		*pa*

109. Pronouns

Words such as *you* and *they* are known as pronouns, from the idea that they replace a noun or noun phrase in the sentence:

After <u>the car</u> left the road, <u>it</u> hit the safety barrier.

The characteristics of pronouns vary from language to language.

One of their important functions is that they indicate who is speaking to whom and who else is being talked about – called "person." So an English conversation usually needs a first-person, *I*, for the person who is speaking, *I believe*; a second-person, *you*, for the person being spoken to, *I believe you*; and a third-person, *he/she/it/they*, for anybody else that needs to be mentioned:

I (1st) *believe she* (3rd) *spoke to you* (2nd).

English has three persons; other languages require more. Navaho has a fourth person to refer to anybody else who gets mentioned after the third person:

I (1st person) *told you* (2nd) *to ask him* (3rd) *to see her* (4th).

The cast of characters in the scene is divided up differently by Navaho and English speakers.

English pronouns vary according to how many people are being mentioned, called "number." The choice is between one person – the "singular," *I/he/she*, etc. – or more than one person – the "plural," *we/they*. In English there is no difference in number between singular and plural second-person *you*. *You are wrong* could refer to one person or many. While number in pronouns seems obvious to English speakers, it is not used in languages like Japanese.

Many languages also use the plural *you* form to show respect and formality, the singular *you* to show friendliness or informality. So a plural *you* may be addressed to several people or to just one. In France, don't venture to use singular *tu* rather than plural *vous* unless you know the other person well or have their permission. Unless of course you want to demonstrate political solidarity: ever since the French Revolution, some groups have deliberately used *tu* to show their egalitarianism.

Other languages count beyond two. Old English had three numbers for pronouns – singular *ic* (I), plural *we*, and dual *wit*, i.e. two people. This is also found in Arabic, *huwa* (he)/*humaa* (they, two of them)/*hum* (they, more than two of them); and Tok Pisin, spoken in Papua New Guinea, *mi/mitupela/yupela*. Fijians count beyond three, having a "trial" form for three people: *au* (I)/*kedaru* (you and me)/*kedatu* (you, me, and another)/*keda* (you, me, and more than one other). On the other hand British sign language (BSL) has signs for six different numbers in pronouns.

In many languages the different forms of nouns show their role in the grammar of the sentence, called "case." Latin had six cases: *mensa* "table" is the subject of the sentence, *mensam* the object, *mensae* the genitive, and so on. Old English nouns had several cases, even if each individual noun used only a few: *scip*, "ship," was singular subject and object, *scipes* genitive and *scipe* dative; *nama*, "name," was singular subject, *naman* in the other cases, with other forms for the plural, *scipu/scipa/scipum* and *naman/namena/namum*. Modern Finnish has fourteen or fifteen cases, a big problem for second-language learners.

The only visible survivors of this case system in English are pronouns:

Subject: *She* went to Spain. *I* knew her well.
Object: John annoyed *her*, and really upset *me*.
Possessive: The car was *hers*, not *mine*.

The differences between *she/her* or *I/me* tell us the main organization of the sentence – who is doing something to whom.

110. Metaphors in Different Languages

When words are used in a non-literal way, their meanings seldom transfer to different languages. Here are some equivalents from English, German, and Chinese, provided by the Newcastle Cognition Group, some being single words, some more like proverbs or sayings.

English	Chinese
a blue joke	a yellow joke
to be green with envy	red eye
blue in the face	turning green in the face
a piece of cake (easy)	easy as turning the palm over
a land of milk and honey	a land of fish and rice
hit the nail on the head	one shot, see the blood
can't have your cake and eat it	can't have both fish and bear palm at the same time
pie in the sky	drawing a big cake
in the twinkling of an eye	fast as thunder
pot calling the kettle black	fifty steps laugh at a hundred steps

English	German
strong meat	strong tobacco
make a beeline for	as the birds fly
under the weather	through the wind
bring home the bacon	the chimney has to smoke/to earn the rolls
a bone to pick	to pluck a chicken with someone
to butter someone up	to smear honey round someone's mouth
to swallow a bitter pill	to swallow a toad

However similar the meanings of words in different languages may be, they are still used distinctively.

111. Pidgins and Creoles

When speakers of two languages come into contact with each other through trade, conquest, or abduction, several things can happen. One is that the speakers of one language learn the other, usually resulting in the less powerful learning the language of the more powerful to be able to deal with them, as Indians learned English in the British Raj or the Anglo-Saxon British learned Norman French after the Conquest.

Alternatively, the speakers of the two languages can try to get along with one another by using something that is somewhere in between the two. This is known as a pidgin language, an example being Hawaiian Pidgin. Pidgins are in-between languages, created so that two groups can communicate with each other without giving up their first languages. According to one theory, when children learn the pidgin from their parents, the language gains native speakers and it becomes a creole. Oddly enough, standard English has some characteristics of a creole. For instance, the way it forms questions with a "dummy" *do* – *You like beer* > *Do you like beer?* – just as creoles do. The high status of French in England for 300 years may have pushed English toward a creole.

The following examples come from an English-based creole called Tok Pisin. This evolved in Papua New Guinea and is an official language with an online news website from the Australian Broadcasting Corporation. Its connection to English is obvious if you read the words aloud. However, the family structure is quite different. You have a different word for your brother if you're a boy or a girl; you have different words for your mother's sister and your father's sister, but not for your nephew and niece.

Tok Pisin Relatives

papa	father, paternal uncle
mama	mother, grandmother
papamama	parents
was papa	foster father
brata	same-sex sibling
susa	opposite-sex sibling
kandare	maternal uncle/aunt/nephew/niece
smolmama	paternal aunt
smolpapa	paternal uncle

	People		Counting
dokta	doctor	1.	wanpela man
draiva	driver	2.	tupela man
dewel	soul (devil)	3.	tripela man
misis	European woman	4.	fopela man
pris	priest	5.	faipela man
kiap	official (captain)	6.	sikispela man
tisa	teacher	7.	sevenpela man
plis masta	policeman	8.	etpela man
stilman	thief (stealman)	9.	nainpela man
masta	European	10.	tenpela man

Knowing which English word a Tok Pisin word comes from is not enough to tell you its meaning. A *misis* is not necessarily married; a *masta* is not necessarily a boss.

The online Australian Broadcasting Corporation *Niuws* has sections such as *Helt Riport*, *Karent Afeas*, and *Yut Foram*. The day I wrote this, the headlines, *Nius Blong Nau*, included:

Philippine gavman na ol group ino wanbei long human rait.

Olympic torch i lusim pinis Argentina long go long Tanzania long east africa.

Bikpela bosman blong UN food agency i tok prais blong cereal.

112. Size Matters

BIG SOUNDS, BIG THINGS

The sounds of a word are not entirely arbitrary but sometimes summon up particular associations. In English words for "big" tend to have back vowels like "ah" and "oo" – *large, huge.* Words for "little" tend to have front vowels like "ee" – *wee, titchy, tiny, itsy-bitsy, teeny-weeny, polka-dot bikini.*

Size (big versus small)

"big" words	*"small" words*	
large	tiny	mini
huge	teeny	pigmy
enormous	little	
vast	wee	
gigantic	petit	

This property has been used by writers to invent new words:

big	*small*
Brobdingnag	Lilliput (places in *Gulliver's Travels*)
bludger	snitch (balls in Quidditch, Harry Potter)
Jaws (James Bond villain)	Tinkerbell (fairy in *Peter Pan*)

Which of each pair do you think means "big" and which "small" in the following languages? Answers are on page 291 – of course, the spelling is only a rough guide to which vowels are front or back.

Spanish: *gordo/chico*
Greek: *mikro/megalo*
French: *grand/petit*
German: *klein/gross*
Chinese: *xiaǒ/da*
Arabic: *quasir/kabir*
Japanese: *kyo/komakai*

I once asked English speakers to decide which of two objects was a *plung*, with a "big" back vowel, which a *pling*, with a "small" front vowel. One object was large, dark and curved, the other small, light, and made up of straight lines. Seventy-one percent answered the large object was the *plung*.

On the basis of these links, the American phonologist John Ohala put forward the Frequency Code Hypothesis. This claims that in all human languages front vowels tend to go with smaller things, back vowels with bigger things. Low sounds in general go with aggressiveness and assertion of power, not just vowels; Margaret Thatcher is believed to have had speech lessons to deepen her voice. The hypothesis applies across languages and dialects; American men are said to find English men effeminate because of their typically higher-pitch range. Even dogs threaten with a low-pitched growl, submit with a high-pitched yelp.

113. Code-switching

When people know the same two languages, they often code-switch from one language to another when talking to each other. That is to say, they alternate bits of both languages rather than staying within one or the other.

Here is a Greek student in England talking to a friend:

Simera piga sto *shopping centre* gia na psaksw ena *birthday present* gia thn Maria.
(Today I went to the *shopping centre* because I wanted to buy a *birthday present* for Maria.)

Everything in the sentence is Greek except for the noun expressions *birthday present* and *shopping centre*. It resembles Greek with a few English words.

Here is the reverse effect in Spanish/English:

So you *todavia* haven't decided *lo que vas a hacer* next week.
(So you still haven't decided what you're going to do next week.)

It looks like an English sentence with some Spanish words and phrases inserted into it.

Such code-switching from language to language is a normal activity in adults and children who speak two languages. Usually it consists of inserting content words from one language into a sentence with the structure of another language, Spanish *todavia* into English *So you ... haven't decided*. The reasons for code-switching are seldom ignorance of one language or inability to control which language to speak. Instead it is mostly a deliberate choice to alternate between two languages to highlight things such as a change of topic or a change in the speaker's role. To be able to carry it off, bilinguals need precise control of both languages, switching instantly in pronunciation and vocabulary.

Code-switching has been used to special effect in poetry such as T. S. Eliot's *The Waste Land*.

London Bridge is falling down falling down falling down
Poi s'ascose nel foco che gli affina
Quando fiam uti chelidon—O swallow swallow
Le Prince d'Aquitaine à la tour abolie

Shakespeare too switches to French for a scene in *Henry V* where Katharine learns English:

KATHARINE: Dites-moi l'Anglais pour le bras.
ALICE: De arm, madame.
KATHARINE: Et le coude?
ALICE: D'elbow.

Henry VIII wrote love letters to Anne Boleyn and Catherine of Aragon in French, the language of courtly love.

Code-switching is an everyday fact of life for many bilinguals. A good example is the online *Panorama* newspaper in Gibraltar, which has a daily editorial containing examples such as:

That's right, y el Picaro dice que he is not going to be deterred, y que he will continue with questions on conflicts of interest.

Bueno hija, el new Governator is going to Brussels to see al quien entrego Hong Kong to the Chinese, que te parece? Simply que cuando venga to our Gibraltar este James Bond and I see him in Momain Street le voy a decir que he needs our permission, my dear.

Researchers in bilingualism see code-switching as evidence for how two languages are interwoven in the mind so that the speaker can switch effortlessly from one language to another, not as a deficiency in their language use. Nevertheless, code-switching still worries the parents of bilingual children who don't appreciate how skilfully quite young children code-switch according to the person they are talking to. And it often worries language teachers, who are instructed by their advisers not to allow the second language in the classroom, thus banning one of the most typical bilingual uses of language from the students' experiences.

114. The Basic Human Words

How much do the languages in the world have in common? It might be that the structure of our minds makes us think in particular ways: human beings classify the world into nouns and verbs because we see the world as objects (sky, table, father) and actions (fly, laugh, hit). Or it might be that we all live in much the same environment and so need words for father, sky, and table because we're not orphans eating off the floor. Either our minds or our environment are similar, or perhaps a bit of both.

Many attempts have been made to establish the concepts that are common to the human species. Usually they have failed because some of the simple things assumed to be universal turn out not to exist in some language: Polish doesn't have a word for "chair" as such, for example. English doesn't have an expression for "appetite wishing" at meals, unlike most other languages in Europe with *Bon appetit* and *Mahlzeit*. Attempts by restaurant chains to invent an English equivalent, *Enjoy your meal*, ring hollow.

The most painstaking search for concepts expressed in every human language has been made by Anna Wierzbicka, a Polish linguist working in Australia. Her list of "semantic primes," i.e. the "irreducible core" of meaning universal to all languages, has been growing for years and now consists of sixty or so concepts. The English versions are as follows. Of course, every word has many meanings in addition to the prime. Some primes are not expressed as single words in English but as phrases.

Semantic primes expressed in all languages
- *I, you, someone, people, something/thing, body* (essentially things)
- *part, kind* (the relationship between things)
- *this, the same, other* (identifying things)
- *one, two, some, all, many* (how many things)

- *good, bad* (the quality of things)
- *big, small* (the size of things)
- *think, know, want, feel, see, hear, like* (expressing how a person feels)
- *say, word, true* (words to do with speaking)
- *do, happen, move, touch* (describing actions in the world)
- *be (somewhere), there is/exist, have, be (someone/something)* (location and existence)
- *live, die* (life and death)
- *when, now, before, after, a long time, a short time, for some time, moment* (time)
- *where, here, above, below, far, near, side, inside* (space)
- *not, may be, can, because, if* (expressing the logic of things)
- *very, more* (intensifying)
- *like* (similarity)

These words are the core of what human beings express through language, common to all cultures and races. But there is a certain paradox about this. The tool we have for establishing the contents of the human mind is the human mind itself. We undoubtedly have blind spots in our vision when we look at ourselves – the observer's effect in quantum theory, in which the very act of observing something affects it. Only a non-human intelligent race might be able to see us clearly.

Answers

5. How Many Words Do You Know?
BASIC WORD TEST

Band A
1. committee 2. strong 3. popular 4. success 5. government
6. house 7. head 8. true 9. office 10. let

Band B
11. ball 12. bag 13. remember/recollect/recall 14. share 15. king
16. read 17. leg 18. receive 19. assessment 20. continue

Band C
21. travel 22. organic 23. councilor 24. glance 25. female
26. discover 27. champion 28. employee 29. suggestion
30. camp

Band D
31. residence 32. finish 33. ladder 34. boycotting
35. conduit 36. yield 37. vacuum 38. portable 39. mining
40. waiter

Band E
41. feminism 42. handicapped 43. ash 44. barrister
45. volunteer 46. vaccine 47. easy 48. transparent 49. grill
50. spa

Gauging your vocabulary size
Make a cross for your score for each vocabulary band in the chart on
the following page. Then join up the crosses. This should give a profile of how many words you know in each band. Usually the curve
will descend from left to right. The size of your vocabulary is the last
band at which you score above 5. If you score more than 5 on Band
E, go on to the Advanced Test on page 245.

Answers to Basic Words Test					
Band	A	B	C	D	E
Frequency	> 1,000	> 3,000	> 5,000	> 10,000	> 20,000
10					
9					
8					
7					
6					
5					
4					
3					
2					
1					
0					

7. Whose Nickname is That?

1. Jack Dawkins (*Oliver Twist*) 2. Lester Young (musician)
3. Canada (rugby/hockey) 4. Artie Shaw (musician) 5. Manfred von Richthofen 6. England (rugby) 7. William Cody (Indian fighter) 8. Louis XIV 9. Wisconsin sports fans 10. Inhabitants of North Carolina, or University of North Carolina athletic teams.

12. Cooking with Words

1. Fiddleheads (fern tips), Canada 2. Pasty (meat-filled pie), UK
3. Candy (sweets), United States 4. Poutine (fried potatoes, gravy
and cheese), Canada 5. Chook (chicken), Australia 6. Garbanzos
(chick peas), United States 7. Etouffée (creole style shellfish and
rice), United States and Canada 8. Skillet (frying pan), United
States 9. Copha (white vegetable shortening), Australia 10. To
shred (to grate), United States 11. Mushy peas (bright green
boiled peas), UK 12. Tourtière (meat pie), Canada 13. Farina (fine
flour), Australia 14. Cilantro (coriander), United States and
Canada 15. Roast potatoes (oven-browned potatoes), UK and
Australia

14. Gender and First Name

	man's name	woman's name
1. Devan	☑	☐
2. Sansa	☐	☑
3. Mance	☑	☐
4. Brienne	☐	☑
5. Cersei	☐	☑
6. Walder	☑	☐
7. Rylene	☐	☑
8. Cotter	☑	☐
9. Daenerys	☐	☑
10. Tyrion	☑	☐
11. Emphyiria	☐	☑
12. Asha	☐	☑
13. Loras	☑	☐
14. Tarle	☑	☐
15. Annara	☐	☑
16. Rollam	☑	☐

17. Alayaya	☐	☑
18. Sarella	☐	☑
19. Clegane	☑	☐
20. Ragwyle	☑	☐

25. Divided by the Atlantic

1. boot **UK** (US trunk) 2. barmy **UK** (US crazy) 3. dirt **US** (UK earth) 4. credenza **US** (UK sideboard) 5. muffler **US** (UK exhaust) 6. bleachers **US** (UK terraces) 7. post **UK** (US mail) 8. diaper **US** (UK nappy) 9. mobile **UK** (US cellphone) 10. busking **UK** 11. pylon **UK** 12. yard **US** (UK garden) 13. grits **US** (UK coarsely ground maize) 14. vest **UK** (US undershirt) 15. gas **US** (UK petrol) 16. fall **US** (UK autumn) 17. pants **US** (UK trousers) 18. rocket **UK** (US arugula) 19. dummy **UK** (US pacifier) 20. gurney **US** (UK wheeled stretcher)

28. Sex and Gender

Italian	M	F	German	M	F
1. *materasso*, "mattress"	☑	☐	6. *Uhr*, "clock"	☐	☑
2. *matita*, "pencil"	☐	☑	7. *Schublade*, "drawer"	☐	☑
3. *poltrona*, "armchair"	☐	☑	8. *Strohhalm*, "straw"	☑	☐
4. *violino*, "violin"	☑	☐	9. *Stecker*, "plug"	☑	☐
5. *chiave*, "key"	☐	☑	10. *Zeitung*, "newspaper"	☐	☑

29. Where in the World Do They Come from?

	Australia/NZ	India	Singapore	South Africa	UK/Ireland	US/Canada
1. daggy (awkward nerdish person)	☑	☐	☐	☐	☐	☐
2. lekker (nice)	☐	☐	☐	☑	☐	☐
3. razoo (I haven't a brass razoo = coin)	☑	☐	☐	☐	☐	☐
4. rutabaga (swede)	☐	☐	☐	☐	☐	☑
5. yakka (hard work)	☑	☐	☐	☐	☐	☐
6. pukka (real)	☐	☑	☐	☐	☐	☐
7. atas (snob)	☐	☐	☑	☐	☐	☐
8. undershirt (vest)	☐	☐	☐	☐	☐	☑
9. kiff (nice, great etc.)	☐	☐	☐	☑	☐	☐
10. toot (stupid)	☐	☐	☑	☐	☐	☐
11. opticals (spectacles)	☐	☑	☐	☐	☐	☐
12. airdash (air travel)	☐	☑	☐	☐	☐	☐
13. prepone (opposite of postpone)	☐	☑	☐	☐	☐	☐
14. kopi (coffee)	☐	☐	☑	☐	☐	☐
15. backie (pickup truck)	☐	☐	☐	☑	☐	☐
16. candy floss (spun-sugar sweet)	☐	☐	☐	☐	☑	☐
17. yaar (friend)	☐	☑	☐	☐	☐	☐
18. ladybug (ladybird)	☐	☐	☐	☐	☐	☑
19. maha (great)	☐	☑	☐	☐	☐	☐
20. bludger (lazy person)	☑	☐	☐	☐	☐	☐
21. chop (to stamp)	☐	☐	☑	☐	☐	☐
22. rowhouse (terrace house)	☐	☐	☐	☐	☐	☑

	Australia/NZ	India	Singapore	South Africa	UK/Ireland	US/Canada
23. skive (abscond from work/school)	☐	☐	☐	☐	☑	☐
24. 'cher (teacher)	☐	☐	☑	☐	☐	☐
25. roundabout (traffic circle)	☐	☐	☐	☐	☑	☐
26. tinny (can of beer)	☑	☐	☐	☐	☐	☐
27. gogo (grandma/elderly woman)	☐	☐	☐	☑	☐	☐
28. pushchair (baby buggy)	☐	☐	☐	☐	☑	☐
29. garbage (rubbish)	☐	☐	☐	☐	☐	☑
30. skollie (gangster)	☐	☐	☐	☑	☐	☐

32. Stuff and Nonsense

Ant and Dec
black and white/blue
body and soul
bread and butter
bubble and squeak
chip and pin
come and go
dribs and drabs
foot and mouth
give and take
health and wealth
here and there
home and away
hook and crook
hue and cry
huffed and puffed
in and out
kiss and tell/make up

kith and kin
Laurel and Hardy
now and then
off and on
on and on
open and shut
over and over
part and parcel
pins and needles
round and round
skin and bone
son and heir
the quick and the dead
time and time again
to and fro
touch and go
town and country/gown
Victoria and Albert

33. Body Parts in Metaphors
(all of these are in the *OED*)

1. You bury your **head** in the sand.
2. You are tied by the **leg**.
3. You pull out your **finger**.
4. You give someone the **elbow**.
5. You can be under somebody's **thumb**.
6. You pull someone's **leg**.
7. You weep on someone's **shoulder**.
8. You breathe down someone's **neck**.
9. You twist someone's **arm**.
10. You lie in your **throat**.

11. You pay through your **nose.**
12. You fall upon someone's **neck.**
13. You speak through your **nose.**
14. You give your **hand** or your **heart.**
15. You cool your **heels.**
16. You put down your **foot.**
17. You have your **head** in the clouds.
18. You keep your **ear** to the ground.

37. English Words in Japanese

1. elevator 2. hotel 3. soccer 4. melon 5. beer 6. cola
7. Christmas 8. hotdog 9. good-bye 10. cat food

44. How Old are Your Words?

"Young" words are underlined. Score 1 for each young word checked. If you get eight or above, you are speaking like a person under thirty; if you get fewer than eight, you are speaking like a person over thirty. Of course this is far from accurate!

1. great	☐	all right	☐
2. bike	☐	cycle	☐
3. crappy	☐	terrible	☐
4. LP	☐	vinyl	☐
5. lousy	☐	bad	☐
6. fellow	☐	guy	☐
7. hammered	☐	sloshed	☐
8. TV	☐	television	☐
9. smashed	☐	wrecked	☐
10. cool	☐	excellent	☐
11. drunk	☐	tipsy	☐
12. stereo	☐	record player	☐

55. Forming New Words

Coupland (4, 8, 11) Pratchett (1, 6) Wodehouse (3, 10)
Burgess (2, 5, 7, 9)

63. Do You Understand Shakespeare?

1. several = "separate/distinct"
2. offer = "to attack"
3. humour = "bodily fluid"
4. hint = "occasion"
5. gossip = "godparent"
6. militarist = "soldier"
7. flesh = "fit"
8. questionable = "inviting questions"
9. graceful = "full of divine grace"
10. rival = "partner"
11. the general = "people in general"
12. investments = "clothes"
13. fathomless = "can't be encircled"
14. mountaineers = "people who live in the mountains"

73. From TLV to IKA

Part 1 internal

1. LAX (Los Angeles International Airport) 2. EWR (Newark Liberty International Airport) 3. IAH (George Bush Intercontinental Airport, Houston) 4. ITO (Hilo International Airport) 5. MDW (Chicago Midway International Airport)

Part 2 short haul

1. MRS (Marseilles) 2. BUD (Ferihegy, Budapest)
3. ZYD (Lisbon TP) 4. FCO (Fiumicino, Rome) 5. SOF (Sofia)

Part 3 long haul

1. HKG (Hong Kong International) 2. TPE (Taoyuan Airport, Taipei) 3. NRT (New Tokyo International) 4. CCS (Caracas Simón Bolívar International, Caracas) 5. TLV (Ben Gurion International, between Jerusalem and Tel Aviv)

75. Can You Talk Black?

1. Who is the baddest man in America? (the President – it means powerful)
2. Is it good for a woman to be womanish? (yes – it means acting like a grown-up woman)
3. What do you do when you're mobbin'? (you drive around in cars to find someone to beat up, or rather "beat down")
4. When are you DWB? (when you're stopped by the police for no offense other than Driving While Black)
5. Have you committed a sin if you're "evil"? (no – it means having a disagreeable personality)
6. Is it good to be straight? (yes – it means "all right, not needing anything")
7. When does the eagle fly? (on payday, when currency with an eagle on it is paid)
8. Who might be your big momma? (your grandmother or a stout woman)
9. When would you get your clown off? (at a party – it means get into the party spirit)
10. If you pimp another person in a match do you win or lose? (win – it means dominate them)
11. If someone has a chocolate Jones are they allergic to it? (no – it means to have an overwhelming desire for something)
12. Where is the Promised Land? (anywhere north of the Mason-Dixon line, the boundary between the northern and southern USA)
13. Is it good for a child to be grown? (no – it means behaving in too adult a fashion)
14. Would you git happy in church? (yes – it means overcome with religious emotion)
15. Are crips good for you? (no – they're a criminal gang found in Los Angeles and Toronto)
16. When are you in the system? (if you're in the criminal justice

system, from arrest to imprisonment)

17. Would you wear a silk? (no – it means a white woman)
18. Is your hair relaxed? (only if it has been straightened)
19. Who is a brotha? (any African American man)
20. Would you be juiced if you won a million pounds? (yes – it means excited)

79. Baby Talk across Languages

1. *kong kong* (Chinese, grandfather) 2. *nyannyan* (Japanese, cat)
3. *kuku* (Arabic, bird) 4. *dadush* (Berber, walk) 5. *lalalal* (Swahili, go to sleep) 6. *shii shii-shii-sura* (Japanese, urinate) 7. *peton* (French, foot)

86. How Do You Learn New Vocabulary?

Can you supply the Italian word for each item?

1. ✏️ ....   2. ✋ ....

3. 🛥️ ....   4. 💻 ....

5. 🗝️ ....   6. 🚲 ....

7. ✈️ ....   8. 🧍 ....

9. ✂️ ....   10. ☎️ ....

Look at the original pictures and give yourself a score out of ten: ..../10.

90. Guessing Words in Context

1. **hantavirus:** a type of single-stranded RNA virus
2. **crampit:** a footboard for a curling player
3. **microfibrils:** very small subdivision of a fiber
4. **annulus:** a ring of fiber surrounding heart valves
5. **salwar kamiz:** loose trousers and tunic
6. **gyre:** a circling turn
7. **illiquidity:** not easily realizable
8. **wichert:** chalk mud mixed with straw
9. **coup de maître:** masterstroke
10. **shift parenting:** exchanging the baby in the factory parking lot when they change shift
11. **disaggregated:** separated into components
12. **stepovers:** low apple trees
13. **rackett:** a musical instrument that sounds a bit like a bassoon
14. **Sehnsucht:** wistful longing

101. How Many Words Do You Know?
ADVANCED WORD TEST

Band F
1. pesticide 2. unity 3. articulate 4. barium 5. salami
6. tankard 7. serotonin 8. obituary 9. gully 10. Catalans
Band G
11. cranial 12. cobra 13. garrison 14. wattling 15. ketch
16. lubber 17. weathering 18. lungfish 19. grandee
20. monolingual
Band H
21. madeleine 22. whittler 23. magi 24. dermal 25. brunt
26. bunker 27. dengue 28. honved 29. proconsul 30. taverner
Band I
31. rapporteur 32. picosecond 33. recession 34. unweaned
35. enfranchised 36. flywheel 37. lapidary 38. judders
39. pipistrelle 40. tilapia

Gauging your vocabulary size
Make a cross for your score for each frequency band in the
following chart. Then join up the crosses. This should show how
many words you know at each band. Usually you will get a curve
going down toward the right. The size of your vocabulary is the last
level at which you score above 5.

		Answers to Advanced Words Test		
Band	F	G	H	I
Frequency	> 50,000	> 100,000	> 150,000	150,000 >
10				
9				
8				
7				
6				
5				
4				
3				
2				
1				
0				

112. Size Matters

"Small" words

Chico	Spanish
Mikro	Greek
Petit	French
Klein	German
xiaŏ	Chinese
kabir	Arabic
kyo	Japanese

Sources

The following list gives main sources of information drawn on for particular chapters for those who want to follow up a topic. Full details are in the references list along with other sources. In addition, the *Oxford English Dictionary* (*OED*) was consulted for many topics.

1. Lakoff & Johnson (1980). 2. Fox et al. (2003). 6. Aronoff (1981). 7. Crozier & Dimmock (1999); Crozier (2004). 11. *OED* http://www.jessesword.com/sf/list/. 12. Lehrer (1974). 14. Cassidy et al. (1999). 16. Algeo 2006. 17. Lehrer (1983); Cook (1997). 21. Rosch (1977). 24. Gachelin (1987). 26. Subba Rao (1954); Cook (1997). 32. Clark (1971). 39. Berlin & Kay (1969). 41. Thun (1963). 42. Levinson (1996). 45. Rosch (1977). 47. Brown & McNeil (1966). 49. Bergen (2004). 51. Wallman (1992); Savage-Rumbaugh & Rumbaugh (1980). 53. Burnley (1983). 54. Barlow (2001); Gottardo et al. (1997). 58. Osgood et al. (1957). 60. McAdam & Milne (1963). 63. Onions (1911). 67. Renfrew (1987); Baugh & Cable (1993); Gray & Atkinson (2003); Pagel et al. (2007). 68. Efron & Thisted (1976). 75. Smitherman (2000). 77. Jaeger (2005). 80. Bloom (2000); Clark (2003). 82. Braine (1963). 83. Lees (1963). 84. Barsalou (1999); Tomasello (1999); Bloom (2000). 85. Mackay et al. (1972); National Curriculum (1999). 87. Gold (1975). 88. EuroCom Centre. 90. Clarke & Nation (1990). 91. Ogden (1937). 92. Miller et al. (1960). 94. McMillan (1980). 95. Tajima (2004). 100. Catford (1965). 103. Murdock (1970). 104. Cruse (1986). 106. Kawasaki & Ohala (1980); Berry et al. (1992). 110. Newcastle Bilingual Cognition research group, particularly Petra Schoofs and Mei Hui. 112. Hinton et al. (1994). 114. Wierzbicka (1996).

References

Algeo, J. (2006), *British or American English?: A Handbook of Word and Grammar Patterns*, Cambridge University Press

Aronoff, M. (1981), "Automobile semantics," *Linguistic Inquiry*, 12, 3, 329–347

Athanasopoulos, P. (2006), "Effects of the grammatical representation of number on cognition in bilinguals," *Bilingualism: Language and Cognition*, 9, 1, 89–96

Augarde, T. (1986), *The Oxford Guide to Word Games*, Oxford University Press

Barlow, J. A. (2001), "Individual differences in the production of initial consonant sequences in Pig Latin," *Lingua*, 111, 667–696

Barsalou, L. W. (1999), "Perceptual symbol systems," *Behavioral and Brain Sciences*, 22, 577–660

Baugh, A. C. & Cable, T. (1993), *A History of the English Language*, 4th edn, Routledge

Bergen, B. (2004), "The psychological reality of phonaesthemes," *Language*, 80, 4, 912–934

Berlin, B. & Kay, P. (1969), *Basic Color Terms: Their Universality and Evolution.* University of California Press

Berry, J. W., Poortinga, Y. H., Segall, M. H. & Dasen, P. R. (1992), *Cross-cultural Psychology: Research and Applications*, Cambridge University Press

Bloom, P. (2000), *How Children Learn the Meanings of Words*, MIT Press

Bloomfield, L. (1933), *Language*, Henry Holt.

Braine, M. (1963), "The ontogeny of English phrase structure: the first phase," *Language*, 39, 1–13

British National Corpus, http://www.natcorp.ox.ac.uk/

Brown, R. & McNeil, D. (1966), "The 'tip of the tongue phenomenon,'" *Journal of Verbal Learning and Verbal Behavior*, 5, 325–337

Burnley, D. (1983), *A Guide to Chaucer's Language*, Palgrave Macmillan

Cassidy, K. W., Kelly, M. H. & Sharoni, L. J. (1999), "Inferring gender from name phonology," *Journal of Experimental Psychology: General*, 128, 3, 362–81

Catford, J. C. (1965), *A Linguistic Theory of Translation*, Oxford University Press

Clark, E. (1971), "On the acquisition of 'before' and 'after,'" *Journal of Verbal Learning and Verbal Behavior*, 10, 266–75

Clark, E. (2003), *First Language Acquisition*, Cambridge University Press

Clarke, D. F. & Nation, I. S. P. (1990), "Guessing the meanings of words from context: strategy and techniques," *System*, 8, 211–20

Cook, V. J. (1997), *Inside Language*, Edward Arnold

Cook, V. J. (2008), *Second Language Learning and Language Teaching*, 4th edition, Hodder Educational

Crookshank, F. G. (1923), "The importance of a theory of signs and a critique of language in the study of medicine." Appendix to C. K. Ogden & I. A. Richards (eds), *The Meaning of Meaning*, Harcourt, Brace and World

Crozier, W. R. (2004), "Recollections of school-teachers" nicknames," *Names*, 52, 2, 3–19

Crozier, W. R. & Dimmock, P. (1999), "Name-calling and nicknames in a sample of primary school children," *British Journal of Educational Psychology*, 69, 505–16

Cruse, D. A. (1986), *Lexical Semantics*, Cambridge University Press

Cutler, A. (1982), *Slips of the Tongue*, Mouton

Edinburgh Associative Thesaurus (EAT) online at http://www.eat.rl.ac.uk/

Efron, B. & Stisted, R. (1976), "Estimating the number of unseen species: how many words did Shakespeare know?", *Biometrika*, 63, 3, 436–47

Eurocom Center, http://www.eurocomcenter.com

Firth, J. R. (1957), *Papers in Linguistics*, Oxford University Press

Fox, A. T., Fertleman, M., Cahill, P. & Palmer, R. D. (2003), "Medical slang in British hospitals," *Ethics and Behavior*, 13, 2, 173–89

Gachelin, J.-M. (1987), "The ultimate purist," *English Today*, 10, 34–7

Gardner, H. (1974), *The Shattered Mind*, Vintage

Gold, R. S. (1975), *Jazz Talk*, Bobbs-Merrill

Gordon, R. G., Jr (ed.) (2005), *Ethnologue: Languages of the World*, 15th edition. http://www.ethnologue.com/web.asp

Gottardo, A., Siegel, L. S. & Stanovich, K. E. (1997), "The assessment of adults with reading disabilities: what can we learn from experimental tasks?", *Journal of Research in Reading*, 20, 1, 42–54

Gottesman, I. (1991), *Schizophrenia Genesis*, W. H. Freeman

Gray, R. D. & Atkinson, Q. D. (2003), "Language-tree divergence times support the Anatolian theory of Indo-European origin," *Nature*, 426, 435–9

Haworth, R. W. *London Directory Exchange Names*, http://www.rhaworth.myby.co.uk/phreak/tenp_01.htm

Hinton, L., Nichols, J. & Ohala, J. (1994), *Sound Symbolism*, Cambridge University Press

Hurford, J. (1994), *Grammar: A Student's Guide*, Cambridge University Press

Jaeger, J. J. (2005), *Kids' Slips*, Lawrence Erlbaum Associates

Kawasaki, H. & Ohala, J. J. (1980), "Acoustic basis for universal constraints on sound sequences," *Journal of the Acoustical Society of America*, 68

Labov, W. (1964), "Stages in the acquisition of standard English," in R. Shuy (ed.), *Social Dialects and Language Learning*, NCTE

Lakoff, G. & Johnson, M. (1980), *Metaphors We Live By*, Chicago University Press

Leech, G., Rayson, P. & Wilson, A. (2001), *Word Frequencies in Written and Spoken English: Based on the British National*

Corpus, Longman

Lees, R. B. (1963), *The Grammar of English Nominalisations*, Mouton

Lehrer, A. (1974), *Semantic Fields and Lexical Structure*, North Holland

Lehrer, A. (1983), *Wine and Conversation*, Indiana University Press

Levinson, S. (1996), "Relativity in spatial conception and description," in J. J. Gumperz & S. C. Levinson (eds), *Rethinking Linguistic Relativity*, Cambridge University Press, 177–202

McAdam, E. L. & Milne, G. (1963), *Johnson's Dictionary: A Modern Selection*, Victor Gollancz

Mackay, D., Thompson, B. & Schaub, P. (1972), *Breakthrough to Literacy Teacher's Manual*, Longman (for the Schools Council)

McMillan, J. (1980), "Infixing and interposing in English," *American Speech*, 55, 163–83

Miller, G. A., Galanter, E. & Pribram, K. H. (1960), *Plans and the Structure of Human Behaviour*, Holt Rinehart Winston

Muhlhausler, P. (1986), *Pidgin and Creole Linguistics*, Wiley-Blackwell

Murdock, G. P. (1970), "Kin term patterns and their distribution," *Ethnology*, 9, 165–207

Nation, P. (1990), *Teaching and Learning Vocabulary*, Newbury House/Harper Row

National Curriculum for England: English (1999), Qualifications and Curriculum Authority

Ogden, C. K (1937), *Basic English: A General Introduction with Rules and Grammar*, Paul, Trench, Trubner and Co.

Onions, C. T. (1911), *Shakespeare Glossary*, Oxford University Press

Opie, I. & Opie, O. (1951), *The Lore and Language of Schoolchildren*, Oxford University Press

Osgood, C. E., Suci, G. J. & Tannenbaum, P. H. (1957), *The Measurement of Meaning*, University of Illinois Press

Oxford English Dictionary, online at http://www.oed.com/

Pagel, M., Atkinson, Q. D. & Meade, A. (2007), "Frequency of word-use predicts rates of lexical evolution throughout Indo-European history," *Nature*, 449, 11 October, 717–21

Prasada, S. & Pinker, S. (1993), "Generalisations of regular and irregular morphology," *Language and Cognitive Processes*, 8, 1–56

Renfrew, C. (1987), *Archaeology and Language: The Puzzle of Indo-European Origins*, Jonathan Cape

Rosch, E. (1977), "Human categorisation," in N. Warren (ed.), *Studies in Cross-Cultural Psychology*, Academic Press

Rundell, M. (2008), "The corpus revolution revisited," *English Today*, 93, 24, 1

Savage-Rumbaugh, S. & Rumbaugh, D. M. (1980), "Language Analogue Project: Phase II," in *Children's Language Vol. 2*, K. Nelson (ed.), Gardener Press, 267–308

Shin, D.-K. & Nation, P. (2008), "Beyond single words: the most frequent collocations in spoken English," *ELT Journal*, 62, 4, 339–48

Smitherman, G. (2000), *Black Talk: Words and Phrases from the Hood to the Amen Corner*, Houghton Mifflin

Subha Rao, G. (1954), *Common Indian Words in English*, Clarendon Press

Tajima, A. (2004), "Fatal miscommunication: English in aviation safety," *World Englishes*, 23, 3, 451–70

Thun, N. (1963), *Reduplicative Words in English*, Uppsala University Press

Todd, L. (1990), *Pidgins and Creoles*, Routledge

Tomasello, M. (1999), *The Cultural Origins of Human Cognition*, Harvard University Press

Wallman, J. (1992), *Aping Language*, Cambridge University Press

Wierzbicka, A. (1996), *Semantics: Primes and Universals*, Oxford University Press

Index of Themes

This book consists of 114 pieces about words, some short, some long. As it can be dipped into or read consecutively, the following is a guide for those who want to follow a particular thread through the book.

Acknowledgements

This book builds very much on the work of others in many disciplines to do with words, as the list of references demonstrates. Like everything in this field, it draws on the amazing *Oxford English Dictionary*, a permanent memorial to the wisdom of the Philological Society in initiating it. Many people helped with the diverse languages it alludes to, including Yoshiko and Goro Murahata, Miho Sasaki, Pam Cook, Mei Lin, Benedetta Bassetti and the Newcastle Bilingual Cognition group. In particular, it would not have materialised but for the work of Robert Cook in researching and vetting the drafts.